Spiritual Food
for a
Searching Soul

FR. JOSEPH BELLERIVE, JCD

authorHOUSE®

AuthorHouse™
1663 Liberty Drive
Bloomington, IN 47403
www.authorhouse.com
Phone: 1-800-839-8640

Published by AuthorHouse 12/15/2011

ISBN: 978-1-4685-0600-6 (sc)
ISBN: 978-1-4685-0599-3 (hc)
ISBN: 978-1-4685-0598-6 (e)

Library of Congress Control Number: 2011961516

TABLE OF CONTENTS

ACKNOWLEDGEMENTS

I WOULD LIKE TO THANK BETH Enos, Maria Parlak, Anna Alastra, Sarah and Patrick Vedepo, Linda Butcher, Delma Santiago, Barbara Fidler and Patrice Robitaille for their support and help in reviewing the texts regarding the publication of this book. I would also like to thank Lori and Sean Heaney for their solidarity and for being the operating minds who, profoundly, influenced me to make these texts public. Sean has been a tremendous supporter who, after reading these articles, encouraged me to make a book for his children. He wants them to have these writings as a strong basis for their faith in today's society, a society filled with many ideologies, even inside the Catholic Church. Relativism has infected the Catholic faith in some parishes where people entered the Church pretending to serve but with an agenda: to change. They want the Church to change its policy on same sex unions, abortion and divorced/remarried people who are not supposed to have access to Holy Communion. They want the Church to be modernized in a world where, today, anything goes. They want the authority of the Church to be transferred to them. In other terms, they want to control their own destiny and not serve the Lord following the path of the apostles and early Christians. However, the truth is that there is only one Lord, one baptism, one faith and one Church. There is one message for all Catholics no matter where they are. The Church is not and has never been a democracy; it is a hierarchy. Jesus is the one who started the Church with a group of twelve apostles chosen by Him. After conferring the Holy Spirit upon the apostles, Jesus asked them to be fishers of men, to go around the world and make disciples, baptizing them in the name of the Father, and of the Son and of the Holy Spirit. He did not start the Church with the multitude because of special training and willingness on the part of these individuals, because they had to give up something before they could join the Church. Those who are baptized become members of the Church who can work in harmony with the apostles and their successors and not form contrary beliefs which are against the Church and from within. So, whoever thinks that he or she can promote his/her illusions within parishes by working with other people to form a defiant entity that pushes for changes is greatly mistaken. These pages will definitely lead the reader to the knowledge of a greater Church, an international and divine organization that is under the guidance of the Holy Spirit and governed here on Earth by the pope and bishops.

Fr. Joseph Bellerive, J.C.D.

PRELUDE

FIRST AND FOREMOST, I WOULD like to thank Fr. Joseph for allowing me to present his book to the public. Whenever Fr. Joseph celebrates the Liturgy of the Mass, my wife Lori and I always look forward to hearing the inspiring and profound messages he delivers to the people. Fr. Joseph has a remarkable gift of making the teachings of the Gospel applicable to the trials and tribulations of our daily lives. His deep knowledge of our Catholic religion and his ability to explain the mysteries of our faith makes each day of our lives an enjoyable journey. Our children share our sentiments and appreciate his keen sense of relating to the young people growing up in this turbulent society. Our spiritual growth as a family has dramatically risen because of our relationship with Fr. Joseph and the spiritual food he feeds us with. He has taught us to be more in tune with the Lord and His Church in order to give a sense to our life particularly in the area concerning our identity. It is a privilege for us to be exposed to such a challenge which calls us to a higher level of faith with its values, its principles and its beliefs. Indeed, through his messages, Fr. Joseph has challenged us to be more kind and patient with each other and for that we are deeply grateful. It is our wish that every person would have the opportunity to be impacted by his broad intellect and wisdom. In addition, with the help of his instructions on the Catechism, we have realized that we are members of an important organization that is divine and international. When we go to Church on Sunday, it is encouraging to know that we are not alone and many millions of Catholics around the world are doing the same thing. We are all fed with the Body of Christ which gives us light to look at our life and strength to carry our individual crosses. It means that we are all in it together and we have the responsibility to contribute to the spreading of the faith until the return of the Lord. This is what compelled me to introduce you to this book where, I am confident, you will find answers to the many questions you may have regarding your relationship with God, with yourself and with others.

Sean M. Heaney

FOREWORD

MANY MEN AND WOMEN IN our modern society conduct their lives as if they were their own creators and choose not to believe in someone greater than themselves as their creator and the creator of the universe. They profess to be atheists while they appreciate the multiplicity of God's creation to be enjoyed here on Earth. In good judgment, it is logical and wise to believe in someone superior to us, one who has created a so well organized place where you find air, water, fire and a nature with the right flora and fauna. It does not make sense to advocate such a behavior that goes against natural law deposited in the heart of every man. If there is no God, why can't the atheists justify the reality of suffering and death in the world? Man can only exist by having a creator. Without this logical reality, it is an illusion to believe that there is no God. If there is not someone who is there as the source of unity in which every man finds his identity and his origin, then there cannot be brotherhood or harmony between citizens. There would not be any purpose for a person to be kind to others or promote justice. The existence of God is the only motivation for man to treat others as brothers since they have one common origin. It might appear very cool to say that there is no God; however, no one has the authority to spread it around because there are consequences in relationship with one's attitude and behavior. It is a dangerous philosophy for the freedom of mankind. With such a belief, those who have power in this world may decide to control other people's lives and treat them according to their unbalanced ideologies. It is the same situation that has caused the slavery of many citizens in those countries where everything is controlled and dictated by a tyrant. For many decades, communism, with its refusal to accept God's existence, has ravaged the freedom of millions in Eastern Europe, Cuba and other parts of the world, thus causing misery, pain and even death, contrary to God's will.

Man is created from the love of God. God is love, and every human generation from the time of conception has to be understood in this reality of love. Therefore, if there is no God, then there cannot be the existence of man because no man can give life to himself. Logically, he has to be created by someone superior to him. In addition, a person would not know how to love, because one can only love others by learning from the source of love which is God. We can be somewhere in the world, but values have no significance for us and for others. A world without God is a horrendous world where you cannot experience bliss. The reality of hell is similar to a place without God. That is the reason why in a culture that denies the existence of God, abortion can be justified because there can be no love where one will give his/her life for the other. Do those who claim to be atheists choose not to see the Hands of God in the world? Or is it a political belief just to be different? The social atmosphere in which we are functioning in today's world invites a need for spiritual guidance in order to respond positively to the questions regarding the last day. Indeed, there is a beginning, and there is also an end to everything. Every human person will know this reality of the last day whether you are a believer or not. The challenge for those who are disturbed about the existence of God is that they are denying their own existence. Without God, a human being cannot be man because he does not have this power to create. God is the only Supreme Being in Heaven and Earth who can create something. He is the Alpha and the Omega. So, those who say that there is no God, do they believe that they are themselves their own beginnings and no one has ever preceded them in this world? If that is the case, they should not be living in this world created by God. They should go somewhere else where they belong. On the other hand, they may decide to call it whatever they want; however, there must be someone who is the author of life and who is also the creator of humankind.

In order for anyone to appreciate this book, the reader must be willing to be curious with the purpose of learning something different and spiritual for his personal growth. The contents might appear to be a dialogue or a message directed to a particular person who is not living his/her life properly, but its purpose is to provoke a conversion of the heart. There is always a better way. Indeed, it will take humility to ponder upon these simple words that are full of meaning for the one who wants to walk in the path of righteousness. They are words of wisdom that can help anyone reforming his way of thinking for a better cause: the Glory of God. However, if the reader is already a "savvy" person who has all the answers and knows everything or who chooses to close his mind in his small world of ideology, there is no need for him/her to waste his/her time.

The following recommendations are keys for a better encounter with the Lord but in a very practical way. It is a way to meet the Lord. It is the Lord's presence that helps us in our daily activities. It is not a complicated message where one needs to take a dictionary or a lexicon to understand the meaning of what is being said. It is important not to run away from this meeting already set by the Lord for the benefit of the reader. Through these pages filled with spiritual guidance in many aspects of life, one has to perceive the message as if the Lord is using this means of communication to talk to us, and the reader is invited to listen. Do not resist Him. Once we make room in our hearts to receive Him, then we will use the contents of this book as a basis for prayer in which we will praise the Lord for His marvels in our lives, we will ask Him to help us transform something within us, and finally, we will ask Him for the strength to carry the crosses of life and to spread the Words. We will not only be transformed by this experience; we will bring peace to those we have betrayed or hurt us. We will become messengers for the Lord because it is our duty.

GOD CAME TO SAVE US TOGETHER AND NOT INDIVIDUALLY

PRAYER IS SOMETHING WHICH IS part of our nature and prayer is important in a person's life. It is like breathing. Indeed, we need to pray every day, but it is while praying constantly and together that we can become Christians. What would a man be if he breathed only once a year? What would a Christian be if he would go with his brothers only once a year to pray? Today, let us all say: Thank you to the Lord for all the marvels He has produced in our lives. He is our Lord and our Savior. Today, let us make the decision to make our world, the world the Lord has so loved, a place where we love each other, a place where we can all be honest with each other, a place where we want to make others happy. Let it be a place where we can communicate with each other, a place where we put our differences aside in order to give glory and praise to God with one heart. Why are we living in this world if not to love? God is the only one who can teach us how to love. Under the terms of the mystery of the incarnated Verb, which was made flesh according to the testimony of St. John (1: 14), all men are entrusted to the maternal solicitude of the Church. Any threat against the dignity of man and his life can only touch the Heart of the Church. It can only reach it in the center of its faith in the Incarnation of the Son of God and his mission of announcing the Gospel of life. In a time when one solemnly proclaims the inviolable rights of the person and where one affirms publicly the value of life, the right to life itself is practically denied and violated, especially at these most significant moments of existence, which are birth and death. To assert the right to abortion or euthanasia and recognize them legally gives human freedom a perverse and unjust direction, an absolute capacity of some groups against other groups. But it is the death of true freedom: "In truth, I say it to you, whoever commits sin is slave of sin (John. 8: 34).

1

ONE CANNOT SERVE TWO MASTERS AT THE SAME TIME

THE CALL OF JESUS ALWAYS implies to give up something, and worse, most of the time it is something essential: father, mother, brother, sister, family, home, etc.[…]. It is a very difficult thing to do, because as human beings, we tend to cling onto earthly possessions very easily. We get quickly attached to habits and customs with which we are familiar to the point of being intolerant to ways that are different from ours. The reality is that one cannot want to follow Christ while clinging to something which does not conform to part of his program of holiness. This may be something in the religious life or in the parochial ministry. Christ asks each one of us to break these multiple attachments, which prevent us from being completely free to achieve our mission. The question is: do we know what attachments are necessary to break and what nets entangle us? Just as Jesus did not retain jealously, its divine dignity to be put at our service, in the same way, we should not hang onto jealously, it will stop us from following Jesus. It is never easy to leave anything. There are always excuses which we consider being right, but to follow Christ, each one must carry out the ultimate rupture according to the will of the Spirit. Certain people will leave all: a boyfriend, girlfriend or even a future wife to become a Carmelite nun, a regular nun, a priest or a monk. Others will give up pursuing careers either in medicine or in engineering while others will devote themselves to the sacerdotal, religious or missionary life. In the same way, the divorced/remarried person or the one who lives in a relationship not approved by the sixth commandment and who wants to have access to the Eucharist, must either give up his/her partner or get married in the Catholic Church. However, for the realization of such a work, it is necessary to start by dying to oneself while recognizing that it is the will of God which fills our heart and directs our lives.

Obedience And Fidelity: Two Virtues Required From A Prophet

WHEN GOD CHOOSES SOMEONE TO be a prophet, that person must speak God's word in the sense that he should open the hearts of his listeners, not only to the love of God but also to His commandments. He should not add anything nor withdraw a comma from what is given to him to proclaim. In a world where some listeners feel that they have the freedom and the right to make false accusations as a way for them to fight with the prophet who is challenging them, that might appear to be a very difficult task. However, both the prophet and the listeners are supposed to be obedient and faithful servants in their own area of responsibility. This is the reason why the Church is consistently reminding us of our duty to remain faithful to God and redirect our lives if we are to know God. Our commitment with the Lord demands sorrow for sin and fidelity to His message. If we have drifted away from the word of God and the sacraments thinking that we no longer need to go to Church because we can communicate with God wherever we are, we must repent and reform our lives. Indeed, God is everywhere, but He expects us to express gratitude toward Him particularly throughout the Eucharist which is our daily bread. To keep the day of the Lord holy means to go and feed our souls on this particular day with the Eucharist. Without this food, we will always have the temptation to run away from the faith and from everything that is essential for our true happiness. Without the Eucharist, we will not have the strength to face the many challenges of life. How many people have fallen into the trap of not going to Mass because of bad Catechism and stubbornness from their part? It is the Church that has the mission to prepare our hearts for a greater cause: to represent God's image here on Earth and to have access to His Kingdom. We should always trust the Church and its prophetic message which is destined to our own salvation. That is exactly what the Lord God, through the book of Deuteronomy, is trying to convey to every one of us: "The one who does not listen to my words that the prophet speaks in my name shall be answerable to me for it. But the prophet who presumes to say in my name a thing I have not commanded him to say, or who speaks in the name of other gods that prophet shall die" (Dt. 18: 19-20). If today we hear this message, we should not harden our hearts. Instead, it means that we must pay attention to it by changing our hearts and be another Christ in our community, slow to judge and ready to forgive.

THE CHURCH IS THE PLACE WHERE WE FILL OUR TANKS

INDEED, THE CHURCH IS SIMILAR to our gas stations where we come to get gas for our spiritual journey here on Earth. It is also the place where we come to show our gratitude to the Lord. When we are grateful to the Lord, we receive in return several spiritual goodies, important for the different trips of our lives in this world. Without these gifts from the Lord, we would be lost. With a particular obviousness, the community which meets in the Church on the day of the Lord is really the family of God. It did not realize from its own initiatives that it is rather the fruit of the love of God who calls and gathers us around the table of his Word and Bread to give us this daily bread, which we all need to live. And yes, it is this bread met in the liturgy of the Word and that of the Eucharist which will enable us to hold firm when we are confronted by various miseries: miseries of hunger, job loss, disease, violence and incomprehension of others, difficulty to love and forgive, and finally, the lack of faith and the relativism which makes us lose the direction of the truth completely. God created the world and all that He created is good, but all that is invented by man cannot be regarded as good. The majority of man's creations, instead of relieving and helping us to be instruments of reconciliation and peace, can wound the Heart and oblige us to be rather agents of division. It is important for us to pray in order to know how to forgive, how to love and how to carry the cross. We have to pray not only in the vocal manner but also in the meditative way where we analyze our behavior in relation with God. We have to pray in the contemplative way where we develop a habit of prayer. We take the time to pray in every moment of the day, whether we are eating, working or cooking. Pray before we start our day, and pray before we go to bed. Indeed, being in communion with the word of Christ can enormously help us to pose courageous acts of compassion and hospitality. To make the choice between the will of God and the immaturity of man, it is necessary to allow the self to be conquered by the love of Christ who will invite each one of us to make an internal conversion. Without this internal conversion, one cannot be another Christ's presence in a parish nor in this world.

THE LORD GIVES US ALWAYS
STRENGTH TO FACE OUR DISEASES

OFTEN, WE INHERIT BODILY DISEASES that we are not responsible for but these belong to the human condition. Genes, which are at the source of our physical and personal constitution and come from several factors and even several generations before our birth, carry those diseases within us, and we are condemned to face them for the rest of our lives. If we do not accept this reality, we live in a constant state of revolt and frustration, and life will become complicated not only for ourselves but also for those who surround us. When we are in this kind of situation, it is important for us to turn to the Lord who will quietly lead us toward the path of internal peace by associating our disease with His sufferings and death on the cross. In this atmosphere of acceptance, which is encouraged by the Christian faith, we will have the wisdom to seek God constantly. Through prayer, the Eucharist and readings of the Bible, He will give us the strength to live with sickness and go forward. On His behalf, we will take our medication as a way of taking part in the construction of our own peace and fulfillment here on Earth. By doing so, our life will be more joyful, and the life we share with others will be lighter and less difficult. There is no need for accusatory or negative attitude which engulfs us in a very unhappy mood towards everyone. The problem is that when we try to blame someone else for our fate, we become bitter and isolate ourselves from the source of life who is God. On the contrary, when we accept everything, we give ourselves a sense of peace. We belong to the community of believers where we find support, and this is the place given to us to truly touch the mercy of God.

Our Mission Is To Speak Out For The Lord

Our faith can bring others to a healing encounter with Christ. If we know the source and the content of our faith well, we cannot keep it for ourselves. We have to spread it around so that others may also experience the mercy and the goodness of the Lord. The determination of the Paralytic's friends was such that they removed the roof of the house where Jesus was preaching in order for the man to experience the mercy of the Lord. In this scenario, there are important instructions for our spiritual journey: we are invited to marvel in the newness of life brought by Jesus and to come to Him in order to receive absolution for our sins that separate us from the presence and love of God. In order for absolution to take effect in a person's life, that person must choose not to go back to the lifestyle that has caused him or her to sin. If we go to confession, receive absolution and then return to the same situation where we were before going to confession, the logical reality is that there is nothing new because there is no repentance and there is no conversion of the heart. Jesus says to the woman caught in adultery: "Go, and sin no more" (John 8: 1-11). It means that something needs to be stopped; otherwise, the blessings of the Lord won't rest upon us. In other words, the Lord expects some cooperation from our part so that His mercy may be fully established in our hearts. Before Jesus restores the sick man to health, He wiped clean the offenses of the paralytic man, and he remembered his sins no more. He also told the man: Get up, pick up your stretcher and go home. All of this is to remind us about the importance of having our sins forgiven. In today's world, where we invest so much emotion in things we do and call holy because we disregard the wonder and the miraculous power of the One who comes to save us, there is the need for us to turn to God and say: Lord, forgive me, for I have sinned. And the truth is that there is no sin on Earth that will not receive God's absolution. The key for us is to be humble and pray that we may recognize the pride in our life. Pride will impede us to see that we have offended God and a particular person. But, God, in His love for us, wants to restore us to Life that is eternal in the same way He did for the paralytic man.

It Is Always A Blessing For A Person To Be Patient

WHETHER WE ARE DEALING WITH God or a human person, patience is essential not only to establish good communication but also to maintain fidelity to the other. A life without patience can bring a lot of sadness to the person who practices it. Lack of patience can lead to separation and cause someone to lose something precious that the Lord has given him. Many relationships have been destroyed by lack of patience particularly in situations where one cannot control his words or cannot wait. It is important to have patience and not to get angry too quickly for things that are manageable. Anyone who is involved in a relationship should always be reminded: This can be said later. It is good to be free, it is essential to be sincere with the other in a relationship but not everything should be said. There are words that are there to be kept only in our minds and not to be expressed to the other person. If said, they may hurt feelings and initiate a conflict that sometimes will last for a long time. In knowing that there are many people who choose the path of holding grudges toward another person and are not willing to forget or to forgive, it is vital to have the wisdom not to say too much. Indeed, there must be communication between people; however, prudence and self-control must be always present in the mind. It is a gift to know what to say when you are involved in a relationship. If not, there will always be accusation and fighting. This is not hypocrisy, rather prudence and wisdom to contribute to a healthy relationship. It is also valuable to understand that your partner is not your confessor. In the Catholic Church, the confessor is an ordained priest who, after hearing your confession, gives you, in the name of the Lord, an absolution. In the same way, to avoid interminable conflicts, it is an obligation to know that good silence can contribute a lot to success in any relationship. It is an opportunity for each one of us to remember that Jesus came to save us by inviting us to choose patience in our relationships. This is the only way we will experience the peace that He came to bring, which we need desperately in this world. He also came to give us a positive attitude, despite our pains and difficulties. It means that because of our faith, it is the moment not to see the difficulties which overpower us like a punishment but rather like a manner of taking part in the sufferings of Christ on the Cross for our redemption. Such an attitude will be born from the heart only of those who want to grow spiritually and who realize that it is futile to revolt against God whenever we have a problem, because who can enter a war against God and have the illusion to win it?

Conversion Is An Ongoing Task

PRAYER IS A TIME GIVEN to us by the Church to improve our commitment with the Lord. This improvement is supposed to take place through conversion of heart and confession of sin. By doing so, we will become the dwelling place where God reveals His glory. However, it is a long process which requires a lot of humility. The difficulty is that progress can be very slow in the sense that it might not be continuous. Everything may go well one week while, the following week, you have to start all over. It means you may be quite disappointed after such an experience, you may desire to stop everything, and not be willing to go forward because you are still committing the same mistakes. When something like that happens, one needs to go to the Lord bowing one's head to ask for forgiveness. Talk to Him slowly and receive His mercy. The Rosary can be one of the different possibilities to learn how to pray slowly. Reflecting upon the mystery of the Incarnation, for example, enables us to remember the promise made to humanity by God through Adam, Noah and Abraham. He offered them all a new creation in order for us to pay attention to God's message which is always faithful to us. To talk to God through the rosary gives us the opportunity to revive the actualization of these promises in today's world, where the antichrist is trying to tell us that we are not sinners because we are all good people. The mission of Jesus was precisely to save us from sins by announcing the good news to the poor, freedom to prisoners and sight to blind men. Jesus came, and He continues to be present in our lives to remind us that this economic turmoil, in which we find ourselves, is the consequence of greed. Therefore, if we want to get out of it, we must build our lives upon His words. We must not take

Him out of our social and political activities. At Christmas, we celebrate the historical arrival of Jesus who was made Man by sharing our human condition in everything except sin. However, we do not just celebrate one historical event; but also, we proclaim and celebrate the real presence of Jesus among us in our daily lives. There, and in every one of us, Jesus is present, but only those who seek Him and who believe in him will find Him: "Where two or three are joined together in my name, there I am in the middle of them".

THE LORD WILL COME BACK TO
JUDGE THE LIVING AND THE DEAD

THE DAY OF THE LORD is coming. What should we do? That is something we must take seriously because He will come unexpectedly. We must stay awake and ready for His wonderful gift because He will bring justice. It is important for us not to take His place here on Earth by judging people. Sometimes we forget that the Lord is the judge and we spend our time judging others as if the authority of this world belongs to us. Nevertheless, the Lord is the only judge and no one else. We all will be saved through the mercy of God. Now, we have to continue responding to His call until the last day of our life here on Earth. In doing so, we will die in the Lord and we will be able to see His face. This is the only way we will have true happiness. It means in order for us to have a beautiful and successful life, it is not about having a lot of material possessions but rather to have the grace of the Holy Spirit to receive and give love and forgiveness until the end. Sometimes, you hear people saying that they will never forgive the person who has offended them. Indeed, under the influence of anger and pride, people can destroy relationships without any shame. There is no way anybody can forgive another person if there is pride. Pride, being the root of all evil, can only call for evil. In the midst of all kinds of wickedness around the world, the Church encourages us not to walk with pride but rather with humility. A humble heart will always be open for a possible forgiveness. A baptized member of the Catholic Church may not be ready to offer forgiveness to a person in this particular moment but he must be willing to do it for the Lord. It is essential that we have a sincere communication with the Lord who will tell us what to do. He is present in the proclamation of the Word. It is the Lord who speaks to us in our Eucharistic celebration. He commands us to take time and pray because not all have faith. Let us look at what occurs in our neighborhoods, workplaces, families, and even in our Christian communities. There are those who come with bad intentions either to divide, in order to reign, or to control. It is our responsibility to become aware of it and entrust these problems to the Lord. We should not panic. We must continue to seek the assistance of God and His strength, given to us by his Son in the Spirit, in order to avoid sinking in despair. Only prayer will give us the force to advance and to be confident in the future. It is through prayer that we will be able to trust others, and others will be able to follow our lead. Prayer is something that a believer cannot live without.

WE MUST BE PEOPLE OF HOPE

IN THE FACE OF LIFE'S uncertainties, we are invited to entrust ourselves to the mercy of God who comes to save his people. We are reminded to maintain our hope in the Lord and keep walking in the faith. Though we may encounter many trials in our lives, we are called to turn to the Lord and put everything in His hands. Where else can we go? Here, we will find strength to carry our crosses of life. One of the great evils of today is selfishness presented under many aspects. Those who claim themselves to be atheists and also who belong to other religions do whatever they can to remove the Crucifix and any Christian symbols in public squares. Indeed, if they have the freedom to not believe, they should respect those who decide to believe and not impede them to express their beliefs. However, the selfish attitude is so strong that it pushes them to think only about themselves. It is something that is able to destroy relationships of marriage, friendship and even create divisions in any parish community. The Lord asks the Heads of State and their Civil servants throughout the world to forget their personal interests and begin to protect their people from all the dangers which threaten them: danger of selfishness and most of all, danger of relativism. Lord, with much confidence in Your mercy, we present these prayers to You. Listen to our supplications and deliver us from all the threats which weigh on Your children.

WE CANNOT WALK IN
THE FAITH ALONE

HUMILITY IS ONE OF THE many virtues that the Gospel is directing us towards in our encounter with the Lord. Being the owner and the creator of the whole world and all it encompasses, the Lord God allowed his Son to be born in a manger. In addition, the humble attitude of John the Baptist in the Gospel is something remarkable that needs to be recognized. That is a powerful message for all of us living in this particular world, inviting us not to choose the path of pride and wickedness, but rather to remain vigilant in praying and practicing charity. Charity is something important for every Christian to live by: charity in helping whomever is in need and also charity with the tongue, so that we don't go and fall into the disease of gossiping. Gossips can disturb the peace brought to us by the Lord and that we must share with others. It is by staying away from gossips that the name of the Lord will be praised with pure lips. We will be able to accomplish this goal only if we decide to stay awake and ready to meet the Lord everyday of our lives, and particularly, at Mass when we go to Communion. The Lord will help us because He is with us. He is present in the proclamation of the Word. It is the Lord who speaks to us in our Eucharistic celebration. He asks us to be vigilant because not everyone who comes to Church has faith. This is the reason why he reminds us that not everyone who says Lord will be saved but those who do the will of His father in Heaven. Faith does require a lot of humility in the sense that we all have a brain. We all are intelligent, but we choose to walk under the guidance of the Magisterium, which is the only authority to tell us how to interpret the words of God found in the Bible. As Catholics, it is important for us to be humble, like Mary the Mother of God, in order to have the peace of the heart: "I am the handmaid of the Lord, may it happen to me according to your Word". If we don't have this virtue of humility, we will continue to accuse the Church of not declaring the truth to us because now we can read the Bible and know how to comprehend better. Without any shame, we will have our own perceptions as if the Church is erroneous, but that we cannot be mistaken.

GOD IS ALWAYS CLOSE TO US

OUR LIFE HERE ON EARTH entails all kinds of events which seem to leave us in a dead end, where, often, we doubt the presence of God in these moments of suffering and pain. In the face of these difficulties, as human beings, we tend to resort to solutions that are fast and even reject the message that God wants to give us through this completely particular situation of our history. The Scriptures remind us that the Lord comes to assist King David. David wanted to accomplish many things during his kingdom, but he forgot that it is God who is in control and started to complain. In addition St. Paul encourages us that we should give glory and praise to God at all times and in all circumstances. In fact, these examples show us how, sometimes, we want to do everything our own way, forgetting the will of God. However, such an act can often lead to disaster. The worst is that our pride prevents us from changing our stubbornness and lack of confidence in God. Instead, we prefer to accuse God by saying that He has abandoned us. The Church invites us all to adopt a new attitude. We are asked to pray more in order to have total confidence and trust knowing that we are not alone, but the Lord is with us. That trust is the obedience of faith. It is exactly this confidence which Mary wants to offer to each one of us in our spiritual journey. In the middle of all the problems we encounter, the Church encourages us to trust that somehow the Lord will come and rescue us.

Be Faithful To The Lord, Walk With Him In His Church

First of all, I want to thank your parents who have made a lot of sacrifices in their lives with the purpose of providing you a good education based on Catholic values. You have been working hard throughout these years. Those are the moments of your life that you will never forget because here, in school, you were exposed to strangers for the first time and to other people different from the ones living with you. Today, you have become a family, and most of you will have friends for life. As you journey in the reality of the world, I encourage you to maintain the Catholic principles and values you have learned with us. They are solid foundations for your future. Be open to learn more about God, about the Church and about the tools that will change a world of violence into a community of love and peace. Within yourselves, you have much potential and many resources, and if you walk with Jesus, you will know how to use them for your success in whatever area you choose for your future. Avoid mediocrity in all aspects, but rather always choose the right path to avoid failures. Respect the process of nature in everything, whether it is love or business. Only that way, will you enjoy the fruits of your effort. Again, if you walk with Jesus from now on, you will always be successful, that is to say you will always do His Will. Be proud of everything you have learned in the Catholic Church, and don't allow anyone to destroy your future by making false promises to you. Keep your heads up. The Lord has reserved something special for you. If you are patient and if you stay away from mediocrity, you will receive it.

Man's Heart Has Been Created For God And Nothing Else

MAN'S HEART IS CONSIDERED TO be like soil in which there is the possibility to sow. When the word of God is directed to that heart, there are many obstacles that will slow down the growth of the word when the devil is also at work trying to sow his kind of grain. However, that is not a frightening issue since the Lord takes care of His soil and He will know how to separate the good from the bad. The thing that is important to remember is that the soil is available for sowing, and if we open our hearts, the word of God will remain consistently in us and will help us to become one with Him. Once we become one with Him, we will become a better person, not only able to get along with others, but also to accept guidance by the shepherd that The Lord has given to His Church. The presence of the Lord in our lives allows us to be joyful people, people who are open not only to those who are members of our own "gang," but to everyone who is a child of God. The specificity of the Catholic Church is that there is one Church, under one leadership: The Lord Jesus through His Holy Spirit. That is the beauty with which we are called to model our Catholic faith, in order to build unity among us. The pope, as the successor of Peter, is the shepherd on Earth chosen by God to lead us all so that we may have access to God's kingdom. The bishop in the local Church does the same thing. He is the symbol of unity in the diocese bringing the faithful to the knowledge of the Truth who is the Lord. So, there is a need for all of us to promote unity despite the fact that we are different. We come from different cultural backgrounds, nationalities and languages to celebrate the Eucharist, which is the source of our strength. It is a blessing to be exposed to such a social reality where we can learn from one another and build that unity and peace the Lord came to bring to the world. There is no reason for anyone to be afraid of those who are from another culture nor to ignore them because we are all in this work together and we are all working for the same boss. It is the Love of God in our hearts that pushes us to strive for harmony. Indeed, there is one Lord and one Church, and we, as the faithful, are many members. To fully understand the meaning of this unity task, it is important for us to continue opening our hearts so that the Lord may help us to put away the selfish mentality we carry within ourselves. Such a poison can only destroy our peace and allow us to be difficult people wherever we go. The reality is that when people are not at peace with themselves, they become rude; they are unable to be kind and be a channel of peace for others. They will always be disagreeable and ready for altercations for no good reason. So, to avoid this kind of attitude, it is good to take the time to thank God just for the fact that we are alive. Let us be grateful to Him every day of our lives and this will give peace to our hearts. We are called to consistently evaluate our relationship with the Lord and those we meet in order to be people of peace and unity. That is the only way we will continue to build the house of the Lord, where there is room for everyone. No one should feel rejected.

THE LORD IS THE ONLY DOCTOR WHO CAN CURE YOU

MOST OF THE TIME WE forget that the Lord knows everything about us: at the time of our birth and also at the time of our death. As a human being, you may go through all kinds of situations that may scare you, but if the Lord has not said that this is the end, you have nothing to be afraid of. Whenever these moments occur in your life, if your faith is weak, you will panic and be ready to accuse God whenever you face some difficulties in your life. However, if it is not your time, nothing will happen to you. So, there is no need to be distressed, just surrender yourself to the Lord. It is only with the help of His grace that you will allow Him to become your daily Bread. The problem is that, sometimes, we think that we are gods. We dictate our wishes to Him, and if He does not go by what we have dictated, then we stop believing in Him and cease talking to Him. How many people have stopped praying or coming to Church because, in their moment of despair, they had dictated their wishes to God, forgetting that we must let Him be God? All of this spiritual advice is a process. There is no way a person can reach this spiritual maturity overnight. It is through many experiences of life, pain and difficulties that a person can become an example of faith for others, if he accepts everything with humility. It means that we will never reach this level of faith if we are still attached to pride and arrogance, particularly in this materialistic world that poisons our brains.

Poverty In Spirit Is The Key To Let God Enter Into Our Hearts

WE ARE DUST, AND WE are living in a world that lets us believe we will live forever. Having been misguided by instructions from some false prophets, we have our private and personal interpretation of the Bible. We build many false kingdoms around us. For example, in a marriage, instead of choosing the road of equality through sharing and offering total love, a spouse will prefer to control everything and treat the other as inferior. There are places where a spouse cannot even have a friend or invite a friend for a coffee; he or she needs permission. There are also relationships of marriage where one spouse talks too much and thinks that he/she is the one who has all the answers. Some spouses will use manipulation to get whatever they want or force others to act according to their selfish behavior. Others will think they are irreplaceable. Is not this an attitude of arrogance and ignorance? In that confusion, they tend to have more kindness, patience and tolerance toward animals and are very harsh to those they are supposed to love unconditionally. The truth is that we have been created in God's image and are the only creatures on Earth, according to the book of Genesis in the Bible, who have been granted this privilege. No matter how friendly an animal can be to a person, an animal is an animal. In addition, based on the dominion that God gave man over the animals in Gn.1: 26, it is not a sin to kill an animal and eat it. This is the reason why we can eat burgers, hot dogs, stake without any problems. We, as human beings, are different and special, for God lives in us. For that reason, if there are people and animals around us, the care must go first to the person and then to the animal, not the opposite. We must treat others as if we were treating God. In other words, we have souls but animals don't. Therefore, because of the logic for us to have authority over animals, animals don't go to Heaven when they die. Only wisdom that comes from the Lord will allow us to understand these mysteries. We will be wise if we accept being realistic and poor by knowing that we are just here on Earth for a while. Therefore, we need to work harder to reach the virtue of common sense in order to understand that you get married to be in a relationship of love and not to be trapped in a relationship of misery. Who says that this particular spouse has to be in control of everything you do? On the day we find the Lord, we will leave everything to be with Him and to remain in His path. There will be no need for us to be in this controlling attitude which, most of the time, pushes us to jealousy and wickedness. What if you awake one morning to find that wealth, beauty, physical attributes and your partner have vanished, who does one seek after such a revelation? God is the one. To find Him, be humble and do whatever He asks you without arguing with Him.

THE KINGDOM OF GOD IS AMONG US THROUGH THE EUCHARIST

MAN, AS A HUMAN BEING, is always looking for happiness, peace, money, power and control. For Catholics, that is one of the many challenges we are confronted with today, particularly in this world filled with new ways of life. The funny thing is that we don't always choose the best for us. How many times will people from respectable families with beautiful values marry someone who they think would bring them happiness? The mysterious part of it all is that they don't always find good opportunities. They are surprised when, instead of happiness, they find a huge and often very heavy cross to carry until the end of their lives. Jesus came to satisfy all the hungry hearts starting with the one looking for the daily bread. He gives us the Church as the place to find that bread. Guided by pride, we can suffer confusion believing we can go to Heaven without filling our souls with the heavenly food that only the Church can provide. The truth is that the Lord continues to nourish his people through the Eucharist. He is the bread that has been multiplied before our eyes, that every person is called to eat. That bread gives true life, peace and happiness. If your parents have blessed you with the spiritual food coming from the Lord, don't abandon the values of your faith for a man or a woman. If you do so, you will have a spouse, but there will be emptiness in your heart until you decide to reconcile with the Lord and receive His sacrament of marriage in the Catholic Church. Such a reconciliation will give you access to the Eucharist, which is the Lord Himself, who gives true life to everyone who seeks Him. It is important to know that a spouse cannot satisfy your hunger though he/she may be a good companion.

Faith Is An Act Of Humility

IGNORANCE AND MISINTERPRETATION ABOUT THE teachings of the Church can lead to confusion and cause us to adopt an unnecessary rebellious attitude, which takes away the peace we should enjoy not only with others but also with ourselves. For some reason, when people decide to go against the official interpretation of the Magisterium on many issues regarding the faith, they choose to enter into a battle that they will never win. Why would an intelligent person want to waste his or her time knowing that he or she is not going to convince the hierarchy of the Church regarding that particular point? To have an accurate and solid interpretation of the faith, we need to understand that Mystery is one of the heavenly spiritual gifts that keep our faith alive. When the Lord says to Thomas, you believe because you see but blessed are those who believe without seeing. He wants to remind us that not everything in the faith or sacraments needs to be explained nor demonstrated in order for us to believe. A good way to build our Catholic faith is to surrender our whole being to God in the same way the Blessed Virgin Mary did. She trusted the Angel who came to deliver a message to her about the birth of our Savior. She did not reason with the Angel. She simply believed. In the same way that the Angel is the messenger of the Lord, the Church is also the House of the Lord, where we should receive our nourishment on our journey to Heaven. The Lord is the one who built the Church, not the pope nor the bishops and the priests. He presents to Peter and his successors the keys of the Kingdom and tells them: Whatever you declare bound on Earth shall be bound in Heaven; whatever you declare loosed on Earth shall be loosed in Heaven (Mt. 16: 19). So, we need to trust the Church officials

27

in that matter and understand that it takes trust, humility and obedience to follow the Lord through the Church. If we think we know better than the Magisterium, and that there is no room for improvement or to learn new things, then we have a problem with self-glorification and resistance. It is then appropriate that we need conversion so that we expel from our hearts such malignancy that forces us to be angry, unhappy and dwelling in a rebellious attitude.

THE MAGISTERIUM IS A
SYMBOL OF HARMONY

THE LORD GOD INVITES US to the Eucharistic Banquet of His Son so that we may be witnesses in this world not only with our lips but also through the way we live our lives. Jesus spent all His life being a witness and accepted death on the Cross to save us from the potency of sins. In Church, there are a number of ways we can respond as witnesses. Our sole purpose is to praise and serve the Lord, nothing else. The altar is not the place where we display and exhibit to discern attention. These days, there are many who want to go there. Some think that there is a power and they want to get it. Others are confused. But, it is essential to know that the altar of the Lord requires some sacrifices. You cannot have everything you want. A Catholic cannot wish to serve the Lord in the Sanctuary or church while disagreeing with the official teachings of His Church or not living the sacraments of the Lord given to us through His Church. Jesus is the one who built the Church. He instituted the Apostles, thus disseminating the authority they received in the Church which aims to serve His people. The Lord has given precise instructions to the Apostles in the way the Church must be conducted and governed. He told them to be wise and prudent because many will come in His name and try to confuse those who are weak. The Magisterium is the official authority established to interpret those instructions from the Lord and serves to assure unity of the Church. That is one of the mysteries of the Church on which we are called upon to build our faith and understand the responsibility of the faithful to trust the interpretation given by the officials of the Church on many issues, such as the Scriptures, Liturgy and the reception of the Sacraments. A Catholic, whether a member of the clergy or a lay person, is invited to free one's mind and one's heart from all those ideologies and possible agendas of the world to enter into this new religion of humility and obedience with the purpose of letting him or her go so as to be led by the Lord Jesus through His Church. The Church of the Lord, as a divine institution, is holy; however, our Church as a human organization is filled with sinners, and one cannot expect the Hierarchy to be holy if we don't make changes in our lives. The people from the Hierarchy come from our families. In order to reach such a level of faith, one must have a personal encounter with the Lord.

THE FOLLOWERS OF JESUS MUST
BE READY TO SHARE HIS DESTINY

IT IS A DUTY, FIRST of all, but it is a gift to rejoice and proclaim the Marvels of the Lord and perceive His presence every day of our life. This will give us the strength to face the challenges that we face on a daily basis. When we understand the nature of our life on Earth, knowing that we are just here for a little while, all of this will change the way we see ourselves and treat others. It is not easy for anyone to accept the persecutions, the problems and the difficulties of life; however, it is more difficult to be humble and accept our challenges in life in all its aspects. We may have the ability to program our lives, thinking that we are going to make a lot of money by investing our capital; but, it is very easy to make bad decisions and receive sudden surprises. That also happens in our personal life. We may dream about having a very good marriage with someone because we invest emotions rather than logic to engage with the other person. After we come to our senses, we discover that it is not that easy. You may have had the dream to have a nice spouse, but instead of having someone with whom you can share peace, you have a warrior at home who is ready to fight for no reason. That person with a warrior attitude may believe that it is a virtue to be like that because he/she is the bulldozer of the house and no one can dare open his/her mouth with him/her. Most of the time, these people with such a behavior will have a partner who is adorable, sweet, calm and respectful, not ready to fight at all. It is a disgrace to be in such a situation; when we are in the middle of problems such as these, it is important to pray for guidance and come to the Lord and ask Him to help us. It is also wise to understand that the help is not going to happen instantly, like

31

when you go to those fast food restaurants where you just press a button and get what you want. The help you will receive is a process and being patient plays an important role. The virtue of prudence helps control the mind so that we don't end up making bad decisions. It is also essential to pray for charity of the tongue so that we have self control and composure towards others. If we behave otherwise, there will be more problems, and this will cause divisions or confusion. Overall, we all need to engage in a spirit of sacrifice to contribute to peace, understanding, love and fidelity in whatever relationship we find ourselves. If we are not ready for stability and temperance in speech at home, there will be no peace. The Lord may have had blessed us with a good spouse or a good friend, but because of our unwillingness to make sacrifices or because of our immaturity and our warrior attitude, we may contribute to its destruction. In the same way, if we don't carry the crosses of life and follow Jesus, we will never reach the level of resurrection which starts here on Earth through unity, brotherhood, sincerity and charity.

It Is Not Easy To Be A Prophet

THE DEMAND OF A PROPHET's life is very challenging. The challenge for the prophet is to deliver messages that come from God, the one who sent him. And we all know speaking God's word in a culture where some people do not want to be told what to do can be very tough, even to the point of making him undesirable. To speak God's word gives us the responsibility for our neighbor's fate. With that, we are reminded that the prophet must speak in the name of the Lord. His message is not directed to one person in particular but to enhance conversion of the heart, so nobody should feel attacked by what is said in the prophet's speech. The reality is that the Lord is so powerful and mysterious. He may know about a situation going on in such a family. And going to Mass, the priest without knowing what is happening will be inspired by God to deliver a message of conversion to that particular person contributing to the fighting in the family. There may be two kinds of reaction: the one who is humble will receive the message as if God is talking for him to grow in the path of holiness and change his behavior. The other one, who does not want to change his attitude, will receive the message as a personal attack and start making false accusations about the priest. But, that is a tactic used by a person who wishes to stop God's work in him. The faith reminds us of the attitude that must fill our hearts in our desire to follow the Lord: to love our neighbor is the key and answer to all God's commandments. To love our neighbor is a difficult task because it must envision the person in its totality, both physical and spiritual. Sometimes, to love may mean that we reveal much and are less quick to judge. Other times, we must give hugs to people to show affection and support, but we must also give them the opportunity for a spiritual encounter with the Lord. Overall, we need to care about many aspects of a person's life. All of that needs balance, and the Holy Spirit is the only one who will help us to reach that level of spirituality in our journey. Let us call upon Him in order for us to acquire the virtue of humility, where we perceive others' successes and achievements as gifts from God and not as a threat to our person.

ACTIONS SPEAK TO GOD MORE
LOUDLY THAN WORDS

THE EUCHARIST IS THE SOURCE of freedom for the Church. It gathers all the members who are part of His assembly in one body, particularly in many parishes where there are several nationalities. It allows us to create a relationship of communion with Jesus the Lord, who is the door to the Eucharist, and his supreme act of love for us. Such a blessing teaches us how to live together in our community with sincerity of heart and welcome everyone without prejudice of race, social rank or gender. Actions speak to God more loudly than words, Jesus insists. We are invited to accept that God's mercy is always there for us, but we have to desire it. We have to recognize that to accept God's mercy means to change our lifestyles and attitudes and respond to God who gives Himself to us. The message for today is that it is never too late to convert. Conversion of the heart and coming back to the Lord are the key for any person who desires to enter into God's Kingdom. God has the last word. The Eucharist cannot unite us with Christ without cleansing ourselves from past sins and avoiding future sins. It means in order for us to see the grace of God in our lives, we must be detached from all spirit of darkness that does not belong to the Lord.

PRAYER BRINGS PEACE
TO THE HEART

THOSE WHO PRAY AND ACT virtuously will experience peace in their hearts. It is always a challenge to remain a person filled with hope, patience and peace. Without prayer, the number of surprises that invade our lives daily would cause us stress and anxiety. Sometimes, we don't look for them, but they are imposed on us forcing us to add burdens upon ourselves. Nevertheless, it is important to remember that in every trial we face, the Lord's plans for us involve peace if you call to Him and not disaster. Being people of faith, we have to consistently maintain our daily prayer with the Lord and put everything in His hands so that He may be the one who guides and leads us. He will be the one who gives us the strength to carry that particular cross and bring us back to the place from which we were exiled. Remember, our God is a God of patience who knows how to wait for the sinner to come back to Him. He does not leave anyone behind. During this particular moment of our lives, let us all decide to offer to others the same treatment given to us by the Lord. The Lord is patient with all of us, let us all try to be patient with one another in order to really become a good witness of the Gospel.

People who pray profoundly every day will receive not only the answers to their call but will also have peace in their heart. The fruits of their prayerful life will be visible on their face and in their attitude in the same way that you can always recognize a priest or a monk even though they may dress with their civilian clothes. So, one way or another, prayer brings something new to our lives.

WE ARE CALLED TO GLORIFY GOD IN BOTH GOOD TIMES & IN BAD

I T IS A BLESSING TO be invited to the Banquet of the Lord every Sunday. Once we have entered the Church, we are invited to give to God our undivided attention through the entire celebration. To each one of us, the Lord has something special to say. We must listen to His message and receive it with humility for our spiritual growth. If we don't, something unusual will appear in our lives. For example, during the Mass, God can send you the message to be more patient at home with your spouse or with your family or to be less judgmental. If after receiving the instructions in your heart, you go home and decide to be more patient with this particular spouse or this particular person, your relationship will be improved and there will be an ambiance of peace in the house. Everyone will benefit from it. However, if you rebel against the message and don't want to change your behavior, you will always remain in that fighting atmosphere and you will never experience peace. The Lord always has something for us. To some of us, He may ask us to have more hope and to forgive, to others the control of the mouth and generosity of heart, and to many others to be pertinent and contrite. All these messages are caring signs from the Lord who wants us to be ready for the Wedding feast on the Last day. Let us not let worldly and temporal elements intrude on us and impede our thoughts to surrender ourselves completely to the Lord. To love God, to repent, to practice social justice, to help the poor, to welcome strangers without any hypocrisy and to protect life at all levels are the requirements to sit at the Lord's Banquet. Let us all commit ourselves not only to take part in the Eucharistic Banquet every week during Mass but also to act like God's wedding guests.

To Whom Do We Owe
Fidelity And Obedience

WHETHER WE EXPECT IT OR not, each one of us will be confronted with a situation where it is necessary to refer to our conscience. We will all, one day, be required to call upon our conscience, which will tell us whether our decisions are right or wrong. In the legal language of the Church, the conscience is the place where the internal decisions are formed, which will result in rewards or consequences in our day-to-day determinations and our relationships with God. How must one react when a conflict exists between a choice resulting from the Word of God conveyed by the Church and the law set up by the State, especially in a context of relativism? The fields are numerous in which such conflicts exist: the conscientious objection in the case of abortions in hospitals, the sale of drugs in pharmacies, the election of candidates to office, to name a few examples. In our contemporary society, either the formed conscience is appreciated and recognized when facing these conflicts or on the contrary scorned, rejected or manipulated. Some think that the conscience, which is indeed a gift from God to each human being, is an obstacle to their happiness and development. They prefer not to recognize its divine source and authority. But those who call themselves Christian, and especially Catholics, cannot serve two Masters at the same time. It is necessary to choose your team. One cannot be a member of the Church of the Lord and at the same time go against the teachings of the Gospel. We cannot do both. The Catholic Church is the organization created by the Lord for our human and spiritual happiness. This is where we can go to receive instructions so that we may form our conscience. It is necessary for us to choose the good way, the one that leads to eternal life. But to make such a decision, it is necessary that the conscience be formed and nourished by the words of God who put the conscience in us and accompanies us on our Earthly journey. In fact, it is such faith that will give us the courage to choose God instead of Caesar.

HUMILITY IS THE FIRST STEP FOR ANYONE TO BELIEVE IN GOD

PRAYER IS A MANNER OF contemplating God and His loving creation presented in a thousand and one ways in our life and of returning glory to Him. It is a form of communication and praise to recognize that somebody more powerful than us exists in our world. It is necessary for all to pay homage to Him for all that He has done because there is no earthly creature that has such a capacity for creation. Some people decide to embrace atheism, which denies the existence of God. It is a kind of pride that does not belong to the nature of man. The reality is that man is created in the image of God, and whoever he is cannot live apart from the love of God, who is creation. Creation is there for man to discover, meet, and conduct life. Whether one wants it or not, by being a member of creation, man is constantly facing God and continuously living in His presence.

To say that one is unbelieving, in the sense that one does not believe in God, is a step that one should not take lightly. How are we to enjoy all that God places at His disposal, the Earth, sun, water, air, flora and fauna, love, friendship, while continuing to think that they are the work of science or man-made? It is a decision that will affect the person's life and will have logical, psychological and personal consequences. Thus, we must pray so as to not fall into the temptation of disbelief. If a man refuses to believe in God, then what does he believe in?

TRUE LOVE REQUIRES A
TOTAL GIFT OF OURSELVES

FOR THE OLD TESTAMENT, THE commandment of love and worship given to the Lord go together. However, all of that must be definite in the love expressed to our neighbor everyday of our lives. The love that must be directed to our neighbors constitutes a sign of authenticity of our love for God and the worship given to Him. There are 613 commandments of the Jewish community that all members must put into practice in their daily lives; Jesus chose to go to the essential. To love God and our neighbors are the center of all the commandments. So, one of the most challenging duties for us Catholics is that the love of God must be shown by loving our neighbors. But the great question which concerns us all is this one: Who is my neighbor? Is it the person who thinks like me, who is the same color as me, who has the same accent as me or any foreigner we meet? This is where it becomes difficult if we have not yet taken the time to identify our neighbor, especially when we think that we will make it to Heaven without any problem. If the Lord has really changed our lives through many years of retreat and togetherness, let us then continue to embrace our spiritual journey by praising the Lord in times of challenge and in times of plenty. The Lord does not require any uncommon attitude from us. He asks us only that we show compassion to all. This is the sign of love that we can express to God, and we will receive conversion through Him.

SALVATION COMES FROM OUR GOD

THE LORD GOD AND THE Lamb are the only ones who know about our fate. There is an important instruction for all of us who are engaged in this spiritual journey towards God's Kingdom. The message is very simple, and it is about the salvation that we all are expecting at the end of our lives here on Earth. The Holy Scriptures state that Salvation comes from our God, who is seated on the throne, and from the Lamb. So, it is important to recognize that we will be saved not because of our merits, rather because of the Mercy of God upon us. The Gospel makes it very clear that God is the only one who can and will save us, thereby, providing a very good reason why we continue to worship Him by prostrating ourselves before the Throne. This means that we need to develop an attitude of humility and reverence to God while living in this world, knowing that God is God and no one else. To believe in God is the first step to asking God to be our guide and allowing Him to become our daily bread, which will allow us to behave with submission. We are called to welcome everyone, to forgive those who hurt us, to bring peace to one another and to share with the poor. We are also called to be humble and obedient to the message given by the Pope and bishops because when Jesus sent His disciples to the mission, He said to them: "Whoever welcomes you welcomes me; and whoever welcomes me welcomes the one who sent me" (Mt. 10: 40). In the same way: *Those who listen to you listen to me and those who reject you reject me and the One who sent me.* This is our responsibility as Christians. As Catholics, if we do things in the name of the Lord, we do them because God expects us to do them. We are called to seek the Lord and His Kingdom. We are called to go to the Lord asking Him everyday to have mercy on us so that He may tell us: Today, you are with me in Paradise.

THE COMMEMORATION OF ALL
THE FAITHFUL DEPARTED

As CATHOLICS, WE BELIEVE THAT Jesus will come to judge the living and the dead, and, therefore, we must be ready for that judgment. According to the official teaching of the Church in the Catechism: when a person dies, there is an immediate judgment made by God, and God is the only one who knows where such a person goes. Because of that, we who remain behind must continue to pray for the deceased members of our family. Based on what the Lord has said: Ask and you will receive, knock and the door will be opened to you. We must continue to offer Masses, rosaries, and intentions so that, imploring the mercy of the Lord, they may make that passage safely. The Lord listens to the cry of the poor. Since we cannot send anyone to Heaven, we are to be humbly begging for God's mercy on behalf of those who have died. Some Catholics believe that whoever dies goes right to Heaven, and because of that mentality, many people fail to pray and even to offer Masses for the soul of the dead. The reality is that each man receives his eternal retribution in his immortal soul at the very moment of his death, in a particular judgment that refers his life to Christ (either entrance into the blessedness of Heaven through a purification or immediate and everlasting damnation). No one knows, so there is a need for Catholics after a funeral service to continue to pray for their loved ones who depart. The Lord has the sole knowledge where each person goes, as it is said in the Scriptures. So, to say whenever somebody dies: I know where he/she is now; is a little too much. Instead of assuming the fate of our dead family members, as if all go to Heaven, please continue to pray for them.

A Sense Of Belonging To
The Universal Church

A S MEMBERS OF THE CATHOLIC Church, we are all in this journey together. Wherever we are in the world, we are a part of something big, which has not been founded by man as it is with many other religions. Our religion was started by Christ. He chose 12 apostles and sent them to spread the Good News around the world. The apostles ordained bishops to maintain the Apostolic Lineage, and from their openness to many other cultures, the Word of God has come to us here. Because of that, as Catholics, we must strive to develop a sense of belonging to the Universal Church and a desire to be willing to be one with the rest of the Church around the world. Nationalism can be an impediment in fostering that sense of belonging to the Universal Church and can disregard the unity and the universality of our faith. This attitude of Catholicity and universality is a crucial point in the faith and we all have the duty to promote it. Every time we celebrate the Eucharist, we have the opportunity to think about many other nations celebrating the same Mystery, hearing the same word and receiving the same Body of Christ through the bread and wine. There is no other religion that gives people such an occasion to marvel the wonders of God throughout the Mass in His Church. The question is how can we integrate this sense of communion in our lives with the message of unity brought to us by the mystery of the Eucharist? This is the main reason why Mass is never a private celebration of a parish or a community alone. We are joined by many others in the local churches and most of all by many others around the world.

OUR FAITH IS GIVEN TO BE PASSED ONTO OTHERS

WE ARE ALL A MARVEL in the eyes of the Lord, and because of this, the Lord wants to open us to a greater sense of responsibility as Catholics. While we are waiting for the return of the Lord, we do have a lot of homework to do. We are all intelligent people: we know what is right and what is wrong. We know how to like and how to dislike things in whatever field of our life on Earth. The job that the Lord wants us to do is to love Him above all and to love our neighbors. The two go together. We all have talents to do that job; however, if we are optimistic people, it will be easier for all of us. We must be confident about accepting this role as prophets constructing the Kingdom of God by being positive. Life is too short. It is not good to let anger and madness destroy our peace, to do the homework given to us by the Lord. We should always take the opportunity to be wise people who spread around love and positive things in order to join in the Master's happiness. There is no time for negativity, because whoever decides to go that route is wasting his time and will miss the opportunity given to him to be ready for the Master of the house, who can't have unhappy people in His Kingdom.

THE LORD REALLY HAS THE POWER

THE FEAST OF THE ASCENSION of the Lord is a privilege that God has given to Jesus for being an obedient Son. After His resurrection, the Ascension was the second gift that the Lord God allowed Jesus to experience. He entered into Heaven to tell us that if we remain in the Love of God and do His Will, not only will we be resurrected, but we will also enter into the House of the Lord. Jesus left the apostles the very difficult mission of governing the Church and spreading the Good News to all so that we may know the requirements that will allow us to enter into Heaven. The difficulty comes from the fact that, as human beings, we have disconnected ourselves from God, who is love. We have built our own kingdom which is made of hatred, hunger for control and friends of violence. Because of this disconnection, we have developed a habit to want everything our own way as opposed to the way of God. The scandal is so prevalent that such an attitude of violence and desire for control is also present in the Church. Certain people will join a parish and think they can act like a militia to accomplish their agenda without reporting to an authority. They completely forget that the Church is a divine organization that was started by Jesus and that there is a hierarchy. When we command things to go our way, we become negative, critical and ready to condemn. If we are humble to accept God's way, we would be slow to anger, non critical and ready to look at our own weaknesses: we are not better than the person we are criticizing. Many times, we think that we are right, and because of that illusion, we lack charity in the way we approach some issues. The Lord, in ascending into Heaven, gave the apostles the responsibility to preach the Gospel of peace and make disciples. Those who listen to them will listen to Him, and those who reject them will also reject Him. This is a powerful message that has been overlooked regarding our call to obedience to the Apostles and their successors, particularly in everything regarding our salvation. Even though we are living in a society that will allow us to be free, which is a wonderful gift from God, we should never forget that charity is first in everything. The law of charity is to be put into practice, not only in the way the Church regards its laws toward the faithful, but also as human beings in the way we use our tongues. Gossip has never been encouraged by the Church and some of us have entered into this habit of talking too much. According to the faith, it is important to know when to talk and also it is vital to know when not to talk. If we miss this opportunity to make such discernment, we will end up having a lot of problems wherever we go. The Lord has ascended into Heaven and this is where He is inviting us to direct our eyes with the hope of reaching the same destination. He is asking all of us to do the same, to ascend, which means to adopt virtues that raise us up and put us close to God.

THE HOLY SPIRIT CALLS
US TO A NEW LIFE

THE HOLY SPIRIT GIVEN TO us at Pentecost obliges us to confess to Christ everything we say and do. He blesses us with many gifts that we are called to give in the service of our brothers and sisters. Those gifts are not only there to remind us about the necessity of becoming leaders but also about the need to be followers. Each one of us has received a gift to share with others. That can be: a smile, kindness, humbleness, generosity and charity. As human beings, we believe that we have power just because we have money, knowledge or hierarchy in the world or in the Church; however, the Holy Spirit comes to remind us that nothing belongs to us. Everything belongs to God. Here on Earth we are just stewards protecting several treasures that the Lord has put into our care for the welfare of our brothers and sisters. When we die we will leave everything behind, and we will go with nothing. This is a good motivation that while we are still alive, we should give God a good percentage of all of those things that we have accumulated and that He has entrusted to us. When we don't think properly in harmony with God, we become non-charitable, and we develop manners where we try to hoard everything for ourselves. We may even think that we can do without him. In seeking God with a sincere heart, we discover however our powerlessness and the shortness of life. Once we realize the complexity and fragility of the breath we have, we will no longer maintain such behaviors and attitudes that show disrespect in the way we deal with others. We will turn to the Holy Spirit who prays to God for us, who also gives us strength and fortitude. Neglecting this surrender to the Holy Spirit endangers the Church's unity. Isn't it easy to become arrogant and proud? May the peace brought by the Holy Spirit at Pentecost permeate our conscience, minds and hearts in order to make us better people ready to preserve the bond of unity between us: We all have one Father.

CHRIST IS KING BUT HE IS VERY HUMBLE

WHAT IS EXCEPTIONAL IN JESUS Christ, the King celebrated in our Catholic Liturgy, is that the Church gives us an opportunity to reflect on the Kingdom of Jesus who is disguised as our poorest brother. The Lord is King, but He does not walk with arrogance and He does not have an overbearing pride and loftiness. He is a very humble King who wants his followers to choose the path of humility in all circumstances of their lives. He was born in a manger. He did not have a private jet; instead, he traveled on a donkey. His reign is a reign of justice and peace. After His resurrection, He left us to sit at the right-hand of the Father. However, He also reigns near us, in this brother who needs me and whom I must serve like a king. With all the homage that is paid to a king, I must return to this particular stranger who is experiencing difficult moments in his life and all the others who are scorned and neglected. It is easy to pass by without seeing them. That is exactly what the feast of Christ the King invites us to do. With humility in the name of the Lord, we will endure anything, and we will have respect for everyone. In addition, instead of regarding ourselves as important people who should not have problems, let us live in the reality of life because Jesus who is a King accepted to suffer and die on the cross for our sins. We too must lovingly accept our challenges in life. Humility allows us to surrender to God for everything because we are travelers in life's journey, and we will all be turned to dust. God is the one who will bring dignity to our mortal body through His son Jesus. This feast is here to remind us how to receive patience, humility and the divine force from Jesus, so we may live without illusion in this world because God alone will reign eternally. Whoever exalts himself will be humbled (Mt. 23: 12).

IT REQUIRES A LOT OF HUMILITY TO SERVE GOD

THE PERSON WHO WANTS TO serve God in his Church must, above all, obtain the virtue of humility. It is the basic requirement to meet before starting to offer a service in the Church, or else, one is likely to cause disaster. This disaster, often resulting in scandal, is not only what we can think of in the realm of morals. It is not the reprehensible act made on innocent beings. The scandal is what makes the small and weak ones stumble in faith. Our prideful personal attitudes in Church can make us stumble in our faith. Desire, power, control […]. Where is the spirit of God in these realities of our lives? It is up to us to be careful. Are we ready to accept the will of God and not to trust our small personal opinions? Are we ready to obey? We are doing it for God. However, if humility is not there, with the first obstacle, we have only one desire: to leave instead of trying again or changing our heart. Isn't that one of the causes of all separations? The reality is that pride, which dominates, will follow us everywhere we go. Instead of solving the problem, one prefers not to face it. Virtues are vital for any relationship or organization where there is interaction between people. It is essential to maintain humility in a relationship of marriage because it allows couples to keep the love alive between them. If not, they will spend days or weeks without talking to each other. The virtue of humility is also vital in a church because one can belong to a community without being the one who is in control. The true servant is the one who can fulfill several roles in the group. Today, he can be a leader, and tomorrow he can simply be a listener and vice versa. Christ is the true servant, because in being God, He agreed to die on the cross. In the eyes of the world, he has lost all the titles and all the powers, but he has gained Love. Yesterday, like today, there were not enough prophets, which means men speaking and acting in the name of God. A prophet is somebody who leads another person towards the good. The false prophet is the one who impedes the word of God to be proclaimed and who impedes the good to be accomplished. The majority of the media does not cease talking about the dramatic history of priests who left the Catholic Church. I will take good care not to judge anyone. I invite you to pray for them. In fact, what is disturbing is the attitude of announcing something that creates sensationalism in the public. They all wanted to be prophets. However, the bottom of their argumentation is only pure affectivity and feelings. We are in a society which sees and judges only with impressions and feelings. In this same confusion, certain people express emotion with one another and make a sensational discovery by saying that they have found love. But how can one believe in a love that does not have compassion, tenderness, respect or patience? Thus, with evil, there is no compromise! With the sinner who made evil, have mercy, love and forgiveness.

A Generous Heart Is
A Gift From God

WHILE THERE ARE PEOPLE WHO like to be praised whenever they give alms to others, the Lord reminds us that our almsgiving must be secret, and our Father who sees all that is done in secret will reward us. Why does the Lord not want us to make public the great things we do to others? The message is that the Lord does not want us to fall into pride, because as a human being, it does not take that much for us to have big heads. If we had to receive praise on TV, radio, newspaper for everything we would give to others, we would think that we are God, and we would expect people to come and bow before us. With such a warning, the Lord Jesus is telling us that in this life we must learn how to be generous. To be generous does not only mean to give money to people, rather to be sincere with whoever you are dealing with. To be generous means that you would never harm the other person, neither with the tongue or physically. It is a gift from God to be a generous person in the sense that the person is loyal, deep, dedicated and good. That person would only do good things for the glory of God and also just to be good to the other person without expecting anything in return. Someone who is generous will always seize whatever opportunity to glorify the Lord by being good to the other person. Such a person is a gift to whomever he/she will be with. God has put that blessing in the heart of every human person. Through good examples, parents can be a source of inspiration for their children, teaching them how to be generous in everything they do. A generous person in the sense of the biblical language can be a blessing to any relationship. You may not have money, but if you are a generous person, your smile, presence, kindness and company can help a person carrying this cross of life. Anyone who is generous does not need praise and glory from people, because he/she is doing this particular action from the heart to please God through the person he/she is helping. There is always room for improvement in our call to be generous in love, either with God or with other people.

FIDELITY BRINGS PEACE
TO THE HEART

IN TODAY'S AGE FILLED WITH technology, wealth and several means of communication, one may believe that the word of God must also be changed. So instead of worshiping the true God, who is the God of Jesus Christ, we may shift the worship and direct it to our ego. In other terms, do we tend to believe that God is the one who needs to change in order for us to fill the emptiness we carry within ourselves? We may even believe that those values and principles that have contributed to the stability and fidelity of many marriages in the past must be updated and are no longer good for the new baby boomers of this generation. The questions: "Why do we have to go to Church? Why do we have to pray and can we not just live together instead of getting married in the Church?" are popular today, and indeed, they are important to those who have not yet met the Lord. As Catholics, we should never go with whatever teaching that is being circulated in the world because the world cannot save us. Anyone who walks with worldly instructions will be lost because Jesus is the only one who brings what the world is longing for: love, unity and peace. So, it is important for us to be hooked up to the Lord in order to understand that our life here on Earth is a mystery. Without God, life does not have much value. The Lord is our shepherd, and that is the truth. For all of us, young or elderly, Jesus is the one who guides us along the right path. If you don't practice your faith, and you don't go to Church, where will you find the right answers to your problems, particularly when you have illness, persecution or death in your family? The reality is that when we practice our faith properly, without blaming God for our misfortune, we experience an internal contentment, and we have the perfect strength to continue our spiritual journey even when things are really bad. This is not a pain killer but rather the truth. This is the faith that has really helped many souls for more than two thousand years and that the Church wants to share with us for our own happiness

WHY IS THERE SO MUCH DISTRACTION IN THE CHURCH?

BECAUSE THE LORD IS THE founder of the Church and His body is one, there is an obligation for the members of the Catholic Church who represent the Body of the Lord on Earth to work and build the unity of the faith. Unity is the fruit of our humility and obedience to God through His Church. We will not reach that level of unity if we don't pray or make the effort not to follow the devil, the prince of division. With this responsibility, the main key is that we must love the Church at all levels and have the desire to be part of it. We must also love its children, even those who are unfaithful to the Lord and are living outside of the sacraments. We must love them with the purpose of guiding them to the path of love and salvation, in bringing them the daily bread that is the Lord and sharing with them the word of God. God is the only one who will be with us at the end of our life, no one else. There is no need to create division and control everything wherever we go. No matter how close we may be to a person, ultimately, we will be alone with God. It is wise not to build our kingdom of illusions without considering His word. We must love our neighbors, not only those who think like us, but also those who are there to challenge us. This is where we have problems in this world. When somebody does something different, we have the tendency to avoid that person, and we waste so much energy that we forget our responsibility to build unity among us. There is one Body, one Spirit, one Lord, one Faith, one Baptism and one God, who is Father of all. Those are the Truths we have to build our lives upon. Once we understand these realities of the

58

faith, we will never act like bulldozers toward the other person, because everyone has received a gift that is destined to be put in the service of others. We are all invited to accept the gifts of one another as a way to celebrate the diversity brought by the Holy Spirit. Jesus Christ feeds us all with one spiritual food, the Eucharist, that allows all of us to participate in building a community through love, patience and sincerity. The fact that we receive the body of the Lord at Mass means that we are in harmony with everything that Jesus says to us through His Church, and we have no other task than to live in loving unity through every single activity of our daily life.

THE NOURISHMENT JESUS
GIVES US IS NOT FAST FOOD

EVERYONE WHO COMES TO THE Lord will not go without receiving something to eat. He is a very generous God, a God who cares about each and every one of us. The food that the Lord urges us to have for our spiritual journey is Himself: He is the bread of life. The bread we receive from Him is the source of strength for us to face all kinds of evils that are trying to scare or frighten us. Indeed, whoever eats this bread with sincerity will never have desire for division nor slandering. Anyone who really gets involved with the bread of the Lord and who has really been renewed by the words of God has to make choices. That person should not continue to promote division nor be a messenger of the devil. When you see people who are spreading negativity around or encouraging others to join them in their task of destroying a community, these messages cannot be from God. We have to open our spiritual eyes, our conscience and our hearts through prayers in order to understand that our God is a God of love. He does not want division at all. He wants us all to be one and walk under His leadership through the Church. That was one of His prayers to God the Father as he was going up to Heaven: may we all be one. So, if you see any hypocrisy or any plot to harm others, the Lord does not take part in it. When you see pride, disobedience and gossip among members of a parish to discredit another person, these actions are the fruits of the devil, who forces his messengers to justify their actions through lies. Often, people whom you never talked to may fabricate stories because they are influenced and controlled by others. This does not come from the Holy

Spirit. They are tricks used by the devil to maintain people in their attitude of negativity. However, our Lord is a great God. He will take care of all those distractions of the devil, and blessed are you when they speak lies because you are telling the truth. The truth is: Our God is love. He is compassionate and merciful. He is slow to anger and is ready twenty four hours a day to forgive us. He welcomes everyone no matter where they come from. When people who are following the Lord are not even open to welcoming others, forgive, be humble and build unity by being charitable. The question is this: Is the Lord God, the one who is asking them to do that? Of course not! You can respond for yourself, and you don't have to be a theologian to understand it. The Lord says to us that we can become new people if we accept Him as the center of our lives, not only to believe in Him, rather to be in communion with Him. He wants us not to be cheap people, but rather He wants us to be generous in all areas of our lives, whether it be: Faith, love, friendship, family, etc.[…]. The food that the Lord gives us is made of several ingredients. These are the word of God, the Will of the Father, the Eucharist and the Mystery of the Church. These are the areas in which we are called to excel in order to become new people. In order to build unity, we must first have the fear of the Lord and choose the path of humility. If not, we will always remain in our pride.

THERE IS NO NEED FOR ANYONE TO BE RUDE TO PEOPLE

THERE IS A TREND RIGHT now where people who are supposed to show courtesy, etiquette, and good manners to others prefer to be so rude that it minimizes their level of education and beauty. Indeed there is no need to act like a bulldozer whenever we are communicating with someone, no matter who the person is. There is a better way for us to express our anger, and actually, it allows us to shine more and have more impact on people by showing kindness toward the other person. In this modern age where there are so many books on communication and so much information on how to relate to others, there is no need to manifest one's power through that kind of behavior. It is a disease that needs to be cured. Whoever has these bad manners should do whatever he/she can in order to adopt another type of personality that is more suitable in this world of technology, allowing him /her to contribute to a world of love and peace. To be kind is also a type of love, and it is as important as giving hugs to those who belong to our group. Where there is true and sincere love, everyone is treated the same way. This is why the love of God is so pure and authentic. In the love of God everyone, regardless of your origin, social rank, or skin color, is treated the same way. In fact, the Kingdom of God is open both to the Jewish people and the pagans. So, if we are Christians who are true and sincere, we should love everyone the same way and not only those who are close to us. If we only love those who are part of our group, it becomes a sect that is not open to everyone. Jesus reminds us that there is nothing special about this kind of love because the Pharisees do the same. It means that as people following the Lord, we have to rethink the way we love. We have to go to the Eucharist where Christ's love is made available to us and where we learn about His selfless love. This is where, as Catholics, we are called to go in order to find the real love that unites us all. Because of the Lord's love, we can't choose to be rude. We are Christians, we are Catholics and we no longer live in the logger's era where people were so busy in the bush cutting wood. We forget that not everything has to be so rough. This is the time of the Lord, and He came to teach us a better way. Let us put it into practice.

WE ARE CALLED TO ABANDON OUR HUMAN WAYS

THE EUCHARIST, REPRESENTED THROUGH BREAD and wine, is the visible sign of the presence of the living Christ in our world. And for us who have the privilege to receive the Eucharist, it is a blessing given to us for our personal benefit and peace in this life. As Catholics, we have to continue our education in the faith, either by participating in retreats, courses, meetings or prayers and liturgies or by taking the time to converse with the Lord in front of the Blessed Sacrament. When we come to Mass, it is important for us to recognize the presence of the Lord in the tabernacle. It means that when we come to the house of the Lord, we take the time to be silent for a while in order to listen to God, who wants to talk to us. By practicing silence, we will learn a lot of things. We will know that there is the need for us to abandon our human ways before we go and put Jesus in our hearts during communion time. To converse with the Lord from heart to heart is the first gesture and posture we should have whenever we come to church. By doing so, we are not ignoring our neighbor at all, nor stopping fellowship in the parish. On the contrary, we are recognizing the presence of the Master of the house who alone has allowed us to live. We should talk to Him all the time and not take everything for granted. He will give us the strength to love and also to forgive. When we take the time to converse with the Lord in a silent atmosphere before Mass, the Lord will give us instructions on how to get rid of any anger in our hearts. The love that He will show us is not superficial, it is rather a love that is universal, deep and sincere. Since we are all brothers and sisters coming to one place to be fed with the Word and the Eucharist, the Lord tells us that it is the way to go. There should not be any division among us. We are a community of believers, and we really have love in our hearts. That love should be manifested and expressed to everyone. Indeed, that love should give us the prudence and wisdom to build the community through obedience to the Lord and His Church. If there is not such obedience and humility, that love is not true love, but rather it is infatuation. We all know that infatuation does not last long. Whenever we face a challenge where emotions are involved, instead of taking up the cross and following the Lord, we have the tendency to run away and encourage others to do the same. The Church belongs to the Lord, and we are just there to walk on the path that the Lord has traced for us in the Gospel. There is no other path. The responsibility of the pope and the bishops is to keep us safe and straight on that path. If, at the end of our journey, we are faithful, the Lord will give us our reward.

EVERYTHING CAN SERVE
AS A PRAYER

AS HUMAN BEINGS, WE UNDERSTAND and know that all suffering is difficult to bear. However, as Christians and particularly as Catholics, we believe that all suffering can be united with the suffering of Christ on the cross. The acceptation of the trials from a spiritual point of view can bring great good in our families, ourselves, and ultimately, in the world to help save souls, including our own. No one wants to suffer. However, when we make bad choices and we fail to receive guidance from the Church, from a parent or from a friend, we may end up in situations that will cause us a lot of pain and sometimes will destroy our own self-esteem. How many young men and women have fallen into traps that impede them to succeed and experience peace in their lives? How many relationships are causing stress and unhappiness in many hearts because those who are involved refuse to surrender to Christ? The reality is that when we don't submit to the Lord through His words and His Church, we will totally be trapped in the world of materialism, where there are so many lies and illusions. We will also become hypocritical. Nevertheless, we must know that the words of God are not there to make us feel good about ourselves, they are there to challenge us so that we may abandon our vices and become holy. One of the many challenges we face today as Catholics is that we should nourish our faith only with the official teachings of the Catholic Church on many issues, from abortion and capital punishment to the reality of hell, purgatory and Heaven. When we all feed our faith from the same source coming from the Lord, through the Magisterium of the

Church, the risk for division among Catholics is less. People won't have the desire to "shop around" or to leave one parish to go to another one where they can hear words that fit them or respond to their ideology. Such an issue occurs when people are not really tuned into the Word of God, such as it is interpreted by the Apostles and the fathers of the Church, and are fed by ideologies coming from the world or from other religions. Such an attitude in a parish can only promote division and turmoil. However, our God is always available to listen to us in good times and in bad. Without such a relationship with the Lord, a cross makes no sense whatsoever to the person who wants to "shop faith" and is that much more difficult to endure. As Catholics, we are called to talk to God, not simply when things are not going well but also when they are going beautifully. We must ask Him for His advice on many decisions we want to make in our lives: telling Him about a problem, a misunderstanding with a spouse or a worry about a child. When we talk to God in a very humble manner, the day itself can be a prayer and a reason to thank Him for being alive.

The Church Is A Mystery

THE CHURCH HAS NEVER BEEN and is not a political institution, even though we, as human beings, try to put politics into it. It is a divine organization whose mission is to bring us to Heaven. The Church allows us to experience the presence and the love of God while we spend our life here on Earth doing our best to practice charity, patience and humility. In the liturgy of the Mass, the celebrant always walks behind the Cross at the beginning and also at the end. It is a mysterious gesture that symbolizes the trust and the confidence that we all need to have in every Mass and also in our own lives. The Lord is first, and we are behind. Whatever problems we have in this life, let the Lord take charge of them. Walk behind Him, and you will never be deceived. It takes a lot of innocence to continuously walk behind another person, particularly when we have been told that we can do everything by ourselves. They told us that we need to be self-sufficient, and we don't need the help of anyone. Indeed, in a world filled with so much pride and wickedness, as Catholics, we must learn to be humble and follow the steps of Jesus. Being God, Jesus accepts to come into our world to share our human condition except sin. He accepts to be humiliated and die on the cross. It means that before we get our face slapped by the realities of nature, we must realize that we are dust and to dust we will return. Therefore, it is urgent for us to do more than just be a member of the Catholic Church. We are to change our heart, because even though its vocation is to welcome the Kingdom of God, the heart is also a field where the enemy sows its weeds. When people choose to be proud, not to be kind or not to follow the path of patience in a relationship with another person or in any other challenge of life, that decision comes from a heart where bad weeds have been sown by the enemy. It is important for us to turn to the Lord and ask for His help to be another Christ here on Earth. Our Lord is filled with compassion for everyone. The challenge for us is to get rid of the habits we have created and free ourselves from unnecessary attachments that have empoisoned our relationship with the Lord and with our brothers and sisters. He is the one who is asking us to change our hearts in order for us to become holy. Our fidelity, which is an act of obedience to God, will speak of God's love not only to the whole world but also to our family, where our children will learn from us and will transmit to others what they have received. Then, we become messengers of the many blessings that the Lord has brought to us.

THE HAPPINESS THAT THE LORD GOD GIVES, LASTS FOREVER

WHEN YOU LOOK AT THE world and see the competition between people fighting to be the first in everything, one may ask if they are really looking for something that can give them happiness. In almost every institution (work, school, home and even in the Church), you see people, driven by an illusion of power, walk all over others to get what they want. Sometimes those involved in this kind of behavior are without mercy toward others and will do anything they can to reach their goals. But how long will that selfishness and jealousy toward others give them fulfillment and happiness? Finally, who has the real power? That is the question we should ask ourselves. When we listen to the gospel, we realize that the Lord is the one who has the ultimate power: the power to give life and to take it back, the power to love and even to die for us and the power to forgive. When we accept the word of God as nourishment for our spiritual growth, reflect upon the fact that God is the owner of everything we have and that all in this world is temporary, we become more realistic about ourselves and we don't give too much importance to our ego. This is known as wisdom. All of us, sooner than later, if we come to the Lord with humble hearts, will be blessed with His grace and healed of our stubbornness, pride and anything that impedes us to be true witnesses. Indeed, the Lord can heal anything from within us that is a source of conflict and pain for others; may His will be done. If we are dealing with any kind of mediocrity that does not show the world the goodness and holiness of the Lord, that stops us from communicating properly with others or that causes us to be negative people, call upon the Lord and He will heal us. The Lord will reign forever because He is the only one who can give bread to satisfy the hungry. For that particular reason, let us continue to give praise and glory to Him.

THE LORD KNOWS OUR
FRAGILITY AND WEAKNESSES

H UMAN LIFE, IN GENERAL, IS and has always been a battle for everyone, even for those who have power, money and fame. There is no one on Earth who can escape from the reality of trials, hardship and pain, no matter if you are rich or poor. Through every state of life, whether we are married or single, there is a challenge and a cross. As human beings, we must be aware of it. Otherwise, we may continue to build lies in our minds, dreaming about something that does not exist. It means that if people believe that there is a place on Earth or a state of life where there is no cross to carry, it is an illusion that is contrary to our makeup as sons and daughters of Adam and Eve. Sometimes, you may even hear priests who, because of the celibacy in the priesthood, continue to slam the ecclesial institution for their misery because they are not married. The reality is that every human person has temptations. People who are single have temptations like those who are married. Marriage does not eliminate temptations. In addition, just because a married man or woman has temptation towards another person does not mean that they are not fit for marriage. In the same way, it is not because a cleric experiences some temptations about the flesh that he is not fit for "priesthood or religious life" respectively. It means that wherever we are we will always have temptations but, according to the faith, we should not follow the devil who is calling us to do his will. As followers of the Lord, whatever cross that is laid in front of us, we should never be scared or discouraged. With the help from the Lord, we can defeat all kinds of evil and hardships that are there to frighten us. The Lord knows our weaknesses. He is near to us. He himself suffered on the cross and experienced pain so that He may respond adequately to our requests whenever we are faced with life's hardships. One of the most challenging elements of our faith is that most of the time we want to follow the Lord, but we don't want to have any cross to carry. Though it is very common for us to cause pain to others through our behavior that is sometimes uncharitable, we never want pain for ourselves. Whenever we have some crosses to carry, we even question the presence of the Lord in this particular moment. There are people who even want to enter into a battle with God trying to blame him for what is happening to them. However, who can enter into a battle with God with the illusion that he or she will win? It means that it is important to continue our education in the faith so that we should never choose to fight with God. Such a conversion would need trust, wisdom and hope from us to always remain in the path of God's will. That is the path of obedience, and Mary has given us a good example to deal with whatever trials we may face in our lives: I am the handmaid of the Lord, may it be done to me according to your word. May we ask God to bless us with a strong faith, not only to profess it but also to trust God in all areas of our lives and to show that trust in the way we practice charity with our tongues and hands toward one another.

THE LOVE OF GOD IS A
LOVE WITHOUT LIMIT

THE LOVE OF GOD IS the fullest happiness anyone will experience in his or her life. To feel loved by God, you know that there is somebody whom you can count on and call upon twenty four hours a day without ever asking you: why are you calling or what can I do for you? A friend always knows why another friend is calling. His call is not aimed to disturb you, rather to give or receive a presence. It is something more than a feeling. Whether we are healthy or sick, we can always communicate with God at any time. It is a guarantee that you will never experience anywhere else, no matter the kind of love that a spouse or friend can share with you. The difference with the love of God is that it is a constant and secure love. It is an inclusive love: all are welcome. God is never tired and never too busy to talk to us. You can always rely on His love. God is full of mercy and compassion for all who come to Him, while we, as human beings, need to rely on the love of God in order for us to love others. Without the grace of God in our hearts, all other love is a lie. You may find true love in the world because many people have been blessed by the grace of God to love without condition. They have been chosen to transmit that love of God to some particular individuals. Those people will be there for you in good and bad times. They will be there for you even if, as a bread winner, you lose your job for many months or many years. They will share whatever they have with you, and they will never criticize you. Indeed, it is possible to find that kind of love whether in friendship or in marriage; however, if you find it, it is a gift from God. And as a gift of God, we should never take it for granted. Anyone who is involved in a relationship of marriage or friendship needs to constantly take care of the love that exists between them. It is like a garden. If you just leave it without watering or taking care of it, weeds will invade it. And even though it was beautiful at the beginning, without care, it will be destroyed. The primary care for a relationship of love is the love of God. We must talk to God all the time about that love, thanking Him for it or asking Him how to make it better. There is always a better way to love because the love of God, which is our model, is a love without limit.

The Devil Also Goes To Church

MANY CATHOLICS, FOR ONE REASON or another, don't believe that the devil exists. They have this disbelief about the existence and the pressure of the devil in our world and daily lives. Despite their choice not to recognize the presence of the evil in our midst, they witness every day things that people do but in no way are the fruits of the Holy Spirit. So, how do we come to the rejection that the devil exists? To believe that there is no devil in our world and in our life is an attitude, as Christians, we would do well not to adopt. This attitude goes against the purpose for which the Lord came into the world. When the archangel Michael was chosen by God to cast the devil out of Heaven, the devil has since been reigning in our world. That is exactly the reason why Jesus came into our world, to rescue us from the power of evil. The Holy Spirit he left us in the Church after His death and resurrection symbolizes the triumph we will have over the devil whenever he tries to deceive us and we choose not to follow his madness. Indeed, the devil has done many things to confuse people. As a spirit, the devil also goes to Church, not to worship God and be submitted to Him, but to win followers and encourage them to do the same and disobey God. This is why, at times, you see people who have just finished attending Mass and receiving communion go in the lobby or in the parking lot yelling at the priest or another person over something simple. They have participated in the Eucharist, which is supposed to give them patience, self control, kindness and forgiveness, but they have again chosen to join the devil. Those are only facts that anyone can fall into if one does not pay attention to the enemy who is walking beside in order to destroy the works of God in our lives. And it does not take too long for him to influence and encourage people to act like him. Nevertheless, when the devil is trying to cause you to sin, in whatever situation or when you just finished attending mass, don't be afraid of him. Just tell him: you know you want to get me, but I won't follow you. It is important for us to model our decisions and deliberations on the Eucharist we celebrate at Mass. May our anger be controlled so that our words may conform to the Word of God, whose purpose is to bring peace and build unity among us.

IF YOU DON'T KNOW, DON'T TALK

To know that to be silent is a virtue and also a challenge for us as human beings. Silence might appear to be something frightening particularly in this era where a number of people believe that they have the right to express themselves wherever they are. However, we should not forget that, as Catholics, we have the choice to do what is right and not what is wrong. We must be free in the Lord to choose to do the right thing and not be free in following the devil to do things that are wrong. Based on the misinterpretation of rights, some people think that they have the right to discuss things they don't even know about. Silence is the virtue that we all need to have. It is something refreshing for good communication. There is a time to talk, but there is also a time to be quiet. In that moment of silence, there are many things you can learn. Try to practice not saying anything inside the house of the Lord if you are waiting for mass or if the mass is over and you are still inside. Pray instead and you will see how your life can be more peaceful. Talking too much can cause trouble either at work or at home. Indeed, it can affect our relationships. Many of the problems between people come from the fact that they talk too much. They talk about things they don't know or about people, yet they have no idea who that person is. And sometimes they are so certain that the illusion they have is true, they even convince themselves as well as others to believe it. But if you don't know, don't make any assumptions and don't give an opinion on something that you don't know about. If you do so, it could lead to gossip. The Catholic Church never wants its children to practice gossip. Our Catholic faith reminds us that when we are inside the church building, it is important to talk less and pray more. The house of the Lord is the best place to acquire that virtue. The problem is that there is too much talk and too much noise around. We all need a time of silence in the Lord with the purpose of listening to what He is saying to us. By doing so, we will have enough gas to fill our tank to continue our spiritual journey. In addition, that experience of not talking too much will definitely help us by reducing conflicts either at work or home and all places. It will give us the gift to discover a spiritual treasure, which reminds us to take God's word seriously and calls us to commitment.

WHO CAN ESCAPE FROM SUFFERING IN THIS WORLD?

SINCE THE FALL OF ADAM and Eve, suffering has entered into the world, and now it is part of our human nature. It appears as something which exists in our genes, and it spreads in many forms and on several levels of our physical constitution. There is suffering that is physical, spiritual, emotional, psychological, etc.[...]. Regardless of its form, the reality is that no one can escape from it. The temptation of the devil is that he wants us to fall into despair whenever suffering comes into our life and to believe that we are alone in it. However, many people try to avoid it and have done whatever they can to run away from it. Some people even fear looking at the Crucifix when they come to church. Others choose to blame God for whatever pain they have and have stopped praying and going to church. And again, some others who are unable to wait and unwilling to endure pain choose to commit suicide as a way for them not to face the reality of suffering. As Christians, and particularly as Catholics, we have been instructed not to be scared of the reality of suffering. We have been told in the Ten Commandments: you shall not kill. That recommendation is directed toward every human person, the duty for him not to kill others but also not to kill himself. So, suicide and homicide are both forbidden to those who are followers of the Lord. Wherever we are, we will always have a cross to carry. It is a thought against the faith to believe that there is a relationship in this world where you won't have any problems. There is always something: if it is not with your partner, it can be with his or her children or with his or her family. You may have a lot of love and communication between you and your spouse; however, the Cross may also come from the children who don't want to follow the faith or from illness. The Church continues to offer us the Cross of the Lord so that we may embrace it with the hope of acquiring the strength to carry our own. Don't rebel against it. If you do, it will bring more misery to your life because the question is this: Where else can you go? The Lord has given His life for us. We, in turn, must be prepared to give our own for the sake of others. That is the only way we will truly serve God through them. The Lord teaches us that we should not keep count on how many times we have given something to somebody. Just give without counting whenever you can. Give also without any publicity for the glory of the Lord and not for your own. This is love, the same love the Lord Jesus comes to show us in order for us to experience peace in our hearts.

The Lord Always Brings Help To Those Who Rely On Him

IN THIS WORLD WHERE SOME people appear to be agitated and ready for confrontation for no reason, it is important for us, followers of the Lord, to learn how to be silent and not feel that one has to always speak. Indeed, we are living in a world where we are free to express ourselves. However, as Catholics, the Sacred scriptures remind us about our task regarding the virtues we are called to put into practice in our lives to be another Christ here on Earth. That is a very difficult task. In our society, the more you know how to control, the more power you have. The more you know how to roar at people, the stronger you are. In the eyes of the faith, that kind of lifestyle is not a virtue, and it is not encouraged by the Church. We are called to stay away from such a behavior. Unfortunately, in many relationships, there is always someone who thinks that his or her responsibility is to control, in the sense that everything has to go his or her way. If it does not go his or her way, then there is criticism, anger and disrespect. The message for us today is that where there is a true love, it can't be so. Instead, love calls for sharing, harmony and desire for unity. That does not eliminate the fact that the husband is the head of the house as our Catholic values remind us. The head of the house is like a shepherd that is there to protect the family and to make sure that no wild wolves come to destroy the unity that is there. The head of the family is to be constantly in dialogue with the Lord so that he may be slow to anger and a good example to the rest of the family. For those who are single parents and who are in the role of being the head of the household, they need to also be in constant communication with the Lord, where they will receive their strength to be faithful. In our day-to-day routine, there is a time to talk but there is also a time to remain silent. If anyone wants to criticize somebody, there is a good time for that person to do it. That time will be given to us by the Lord, especially if we rely on Him. When we talk to the Lord in a constant manner, sometimes we will discover that the Lord has given us another idea or another attitude where we no longer see the problem that was originally there. However, when a person does not have this particular encounter with the Lord, he or she is quick to express anger and be impatient. We all can learn from God who is slow to anger and full of compassion. Don't let your anger push you to say things that are disrespectful and aimed at starting a fight. That is not the fruit of freedom but rather being a slave to evil.

Your Love Toward The Other Should Not Be Costless

MANY PEOPLE TALK ABOUT LOVE and almost everyone has someone that he or she loves: a spouse, a parent or a friend. However, the love we give to the other person depends on the amount of generosity that one may have in his or her heart. In some relationships, it appears to be an unbalanced love that sometimes creates a lot of distraction and brings doubt to the heart of the one who thinks that he or she is giving too much. But we have to understand that there are people who really have love in their hearts for another person but have no concept of how to express it. They just don't know how to put seasoning in it. This all depends on the way they were brought up. If you grow up in a family where your parents show affection to one another, the kids will learn to express love when they become adults and will do the same toward their spouses or friends. But if they were raised in a home where the atmosphere was like a funeral home, where affection is not expressed or is considered to be unclean, then when the kids become adults, they will convey the same funeral home atmosphere to their respective relationships. Nevertheless, if we were raised in a family where there were a lot of hugs, as we continue to grow in the faith, we can learn a lot from the Lord and give the best of ourselves to the other person. We are supposed to be generous people, not only ready to give to others but also open to receive from others, which is where we have problems. Pride will impede us sometimes to reach that level of generosity, which is an attitude of humility that is important for us to have. God does not need anything from us, but His humility is unbelievable.

Remember how He accepted the generosity of the poor widow, and He praised her attitude for having great love in her heart in giving all she had? Her love for God was not inferior but a strong and sincere love. She gave without counting because she was not stingy. When people choose to be superficial, everything they give is insincere: their love, their friendship, their smile, etc. They call you friends today and the next day because of some disagreement, they choose not to talk to you. Jesus rejects that kind of attitude because He expects that we forgive the person who has hurt us. He prefers unity and peace above all. He calls us to be generous to others, not only in quantity but also in quality where there is no hypocrisy. In addition, you don't have to dig deep before you get some response from the other person. It requires a lot of generosity of heart for a person to love others in the way Jesus loves us.

DON'T DWELL TOO MUCH ON YOURSELF

THE LORD CREATED US AS human beings not to live isolated from one another, rather to support one another and work together for the common good of all. Nobody can live independently and away from the rest of the world. We all need interaction with others to find the balance of our being and complete the fullness of our human nature. With this positive interdependence for our well being, we are all capable of dialogue and sharing with everyone without, however, ceding to the fashions of relativism. The problem is that there is some delusional mentality that tells us: do everything by ourselves and that we don't need anybody to help us. Is that not the reason why sometimes you see people who, lost when driving, prefer to waste their time going around in circles to figure it out instead of stopping for two minutes to ask for directions? We may believe that we don't need people or we don't need any advice from anybody. The pretenses we have sometimes are incredible, and the devil likes playing with our ambitions. Who can be really self-sufficient in this world? No one. If you have money, you need to go and buy food, and if you want to boil your money to be self-sufficient, you need to buy a pan. So, you have to go to someone in order to complete what you have. To believe that you are self-sufficient is a lie. As we grow in our spiritual journey, with the help of the Holy Spirit, we are able to discover that we are to watch our self complacency. We have to be transparent in the sense that we should be able to laugh at ourselves, not because we are losing it or we are crazy, rather because there is a lot of falsity when we start trusting ourselves and distrust the Lord and His Church. When we fool ourselves with misconceptions, the sense of truthfulness is not there, and we become superficial people. When we are true to ourselves, our love for others becomes sincere and there is no hypocrisy within us. Who are we? Don't pretend to be someone else when we are all mortals. The reality of our being will be revealed on the last day, the Day of Judgment, when the Lord will come. This is why we should go and reflect upon the shortness of life in order to have the appropriate behavior while we are still alive. There should be complete harmony on our part, between the faith and the teachings of the Lord delivered by the Church. Otherwise, we are engaging in a losing battle that is the fruit of our pride and stubbornness. It is necessary for us not to fight with the faith or the Church in order to teach future generations something valid, solid rules for behavior capable of indicating the path toward which the young or the adult should decisively order his life.

HOLINESS AND DEATH, TWO REALITIES OF OUR FAITH AND LIFE

THE LITURGY OF THE MASS we celebrate everyday or every weekend draws us all to something that is true, good, beautiful and one. God is the only one who can offer such elements of life for our personal growth. Truth, goodness, beauty and unity are all things that lift us up to something which makes us happy, especially when you can find them all in a husband, a wife, a friend, etc. How much more true happiness will we experience in the presence of the Lord who represents the four elements mentioned above? Those virtues which identify the personality of God are also important for us to have in our lives so that we may live them and transmit them to those living around us. The saints whose feasts we celebrate in our Liturgy remind us constantly about the importance and need to allow ourselves to give thanks to God for everything. The communion of saints, who dedicated their lives to glorify and worship the Lord, is a reminder that our primary role as creatures and Christians is to praise God. To praise God means to be in communion with the rest of the Church present here in the diocese, in this country and around the world. When we stand in the Church facing the tabernacle, the Crucifix and the altar, we are witnesses of something powerful and big. Our problem is that when we are trapped in our little world, we become so attached to what we are accustomed to that we miss the truth, goodness, beauty and unity in all that we are celebrating. This is why the liturgy is calling us to die to ourselves and be born again in the Lord with the purpose of having the proper outfit to be part of this family whenever we present ourselves to the Lord. We are a chosen race by the grace of God and we must be in communion with one another to those both visible and invisible. It takes humility to be a saint because we must depend on someone who is greater than us. We must pray for the living and dead, and that is how we express our communion of saints. We should never assume that our relatives are in Heaven, and therefore, there is no need for us to pray for them. We have to pray for them and request God's mercy upon them. Ultimately, God is the only one who knows where they are. And since we don't know, we have to be humble by bending our knees begging the Lord for their salvation. We must be in communion with them until the end of time, when the Lord will return in His Glory.

JESUS, A KING WHO
SHARES OUR HUMANITY

CATHOLICS OF ALL PARISHES AROUND the world are invited to meditate over Jesus, who is presented in the Liturgy as the King of the universe. This meditation is important for our faith because it allows us to amend things that need to be amended in our lives, particularly in our relationship with God and our brothers and sisters. Jesus Christ is the King of kings, who was born in a manger and who accepted to die on the cross to show us how to love and the path that leads to salvation. Jesus is King, but He preferred to live a humble lifestyle among the poor in spirit contrary to the kings living in this world separated from the rest of the people. It might be difficult for us to comprehend all of this; however, it is a powerful message for our spiritual growth where most people tend to see material possessions as a blessing to them and their family. The Kingdom of Jesus offers to us the possibility to live in this world with contentment and peace, even though we may not have a lot of wealth. As believers, nothing disturbs us because we are never alone in our pains. The Lord is always there to support us. However, we must understand that every human person on Earth has a cross to carry. Every father or mother converses with the Lord about something that is not going well in the family. A person may have all the wealth of the Earth; however, this does not mean that he or she is exempt from pains and problems in his or her life. There are many kinds of trials and hardships for a human person. They are situated at different levels, and it is essential that we turn to the Lord to receive strength that will encourage us to keep going. We must walk with the Lord in order to be protected. We must rely on God for everything concerning our present and future. If we do not look for the Lord and His help, our problems stay unresolved, and we put ourselves in situations that bring more problems. We should not do that because we have to love ourselves. The enigma is the following: if we don't love ourselves and if we don't know how to treat ourselves properly, how can we expect to love another person? If we mistreat ourselves, we won't know how to bring love to others. Many people have forgotten that they must learn first how to love themselves, but they rely on someone else to love them. When we are involved in a relationship looking for someone to love us, this relationship won't last very long. You can only maintain love through love. It means that we must learn how to forgive in order to move forward with the purpose of establishing peace and unity. Is this not one of our many dilemmas in this world of today? Jesus, as King, knew how to give the best to himself: In everything that was happening to Him, he always said to the Father: Thy will be done. He knew how to endure all kinds of hardships. He knew how to carry His cross. He did not blame God, His father for what was happening to Him. He did not stop talking to God for His misfortune. In this way, He acted as a true Son. He is the King because no one else has ever done this before. Christ has done a lot of things for us by showing us another way to deal with sufferings. He surrendered himself totally to God, His Father and that is what we are called upon to do: to have a lot of respect for God, to call upon Him and to put everything into His hands. May our eyes be opened to the Light revealed by the King, so that in the midst of the tragedies and challenges present in our lives, we conform our thoughts and sentiments to the humility of Christ.

WE MUST BE TRUE TO GOD
AND TO EACH OTHER

THE WORDS OF GOD INVITE us always to think about the place of holiness in our life. One of the areas that needs without any doubt a conversion of the heart is the area of money, the existence of rich and poor, the importance of sincerity and honesty in our relationships with each other, and finally the need to choose God rather than money. When the prophet Amos was living on earth, he discovered that there are not only unequal relationships between various social groups of the community, but there were also people who got rich exploiting the poor. These people looked forward to the end of Sabbath to sell their products at exorbitant prices, and worse, they deceived their customers by falsifying the balances. Recognizing this abuse in the community of Israel, the prophet expresses his displeasure by denouncing these hypocritical attitudes, illustrating their harm and injustice committed to the poor. In our spiritual journey, we must show the importance of justice, charity and sharing in our midst in order to build the Kingdom of God. The prophet Amos tells us that there is a very close relationship between faith and our actions in our relationships with each other. We cannot truly love God if we do not like our neighbors. But the problem facing us all as human beings is that we have difficulty in identifying the neighbor. Who is my neighbor? This is the fundamental question that arises in spirituality. My neighbor is he who thinks like me? Is he the one who is my color? Where I work, do I contribute to the justice and happiness of others, or do I sow division because of my selfishness and my hypocrisy? Therefore, one must think of these superficial relationships where sometimes you think you have a friend in front of you who gives you a smile, but who, from behind, launches a knife. These types of defects cannot build harmony and trust in a relationship, whether friendly, marital, family or communal. And when there is no trust and honesty in a relationship, true love cannot exist. As Christians, we must pray to the Lord so that this poison does not enter into our heart. The worst thing that can happen to us is to believe that we have nothing for which to reproach ourselves. To enter into the intimate heart of Jesus, we must recognize that we are sinners, penitent sinners, humble sinners who rely on the mercy of God and not on our own achievements. This can be realized through the virtue of humility. Humility is to acknowledge our limitations and let God enter into our lives to heal us, give us strength and courage in difficult times. Instead of falling in continual revolt, let God win the battle. For that, like Mary, we may say: May it be done to me according to your word. How do we react when we learn that we have only six months to live? How do we accept that we are suffering from cancer and that we will die and leave our property, our families, our bank accounts? Being humble is watching each of our brothers and sisters with a look of tenderness, a tenderness on his countenance as he beholds the most lost ones ready to die for them. Humility is not only the conversion to love, it is also this encounter with our Savior. When we reach spiritual maturity, this stage of life where we let God be the master of our lives, we will not need to be selfish, aggressive and uncaring. We will all become the kind of people described by St. Paul's first letter to Timothy : "These are the things you must preach and teach. Whoever teaches in any other way, not holding to the sound doctrines of our Lord Jesus Christ and the teaching proper to true religion, should be recognized as both conceited and ignorant, a sick man in his passion for polemics and controversy. From these come envy, dissension, slander, evil suspicion in a word, the bickering of men with twisted minds who have lost all sense of truth. Such men value religion only as a means of personal gain(1Tm: 6, 2-5)". A community leader should be perfect: opening his house to all, able to teach, a non-drinker, not violent but serene, peaceful and disinterested. This is a message for us all, a moving message inviting us in prayer to an awareness of our weaknesses. We have to present these weaknesses to the Lord for whom nothing is impossible. We are not supposed to say "this is how I am, I cannot change". We cannot be Christians who lock themselves in their little boxes, forgetting the misery of others. We must pray for others who have preceded us and those who are still alive. Pray for those who persecute us and those who have hurt us. Pray for those who are not kind and patient with us. If you have a husband or wife who lacks patience and does not want to take time to communicate and share, or someone who gets mad for nothing, pray for him. The Church wants to remind us of the power of prayer requests. Jesus wants us to be perfect as our Father! How is this possible? Jesus knows the Father's heart and attaches such importance to the brotherly love that He admonishes us to leave our gift before the altar and to go reconcile with our brother. He says all this because he wants us to be happy. The happiness he promised us is not in the things of this world, neither in power nor in the titles, nor glory, nor jealousy or selfishness in which we fall oftentimes. Happiness resides in doing the will of God. What is surprising is we forget that in our coffins, we carry with us no money, no house, no beautiful cars, not even our husband or wife. It is something outrageous: divisions, competitions, illusions, hypocrisy. All those forms of selfishness have no reason to be.

THE CHURCH CONTINUES TO
FACE MULTIPLE CHALLENGES

THERE ARE MANY PROBLEMS IN the world of today: poverty, unemployment, dictatorships, injustice, abuse, secularism. Increasingly, we are witnessing a rise of leftism, fanaticism and fundamentalism forcing followers to become vulgar, barbarous, indifferent and intolerant. We live in a world where people tend to be rather selfish and this situation is being seen at all levels of society. On one side there is the rich West that wants peace, but seems to be deaf to the cries of the poor and on the other side the third world victims of dictatorships and totalitarian systems claim justice but in their impatience, they use violence. In addition, we are also witnessing situations where governments leaders manipulating the social imbalance in society present themselves as friends of the poor and enemies of the rich with the purpose of gaining power and remain in it as dictators who take away the freedom of individuals. So, we are invited to pray at every Eucharist that the Church manages to find the words, the means and facilities for the proclamation of the Gospel with the purpose of leading the faithful towards love. This is not an easy task. We have seen in the last decade how man is a being capable of anything. This is someone who can do everything both in the field of love and in the field of evil even if that person claims to serve God. Regardless of social status, you'll meet people who are able to love, to be sincere, and you'll meet others who are full of vices, hypocrisy and who prefer to do evil instead of doing good. It is to this man that the Church is called to proclaim the word of God. It is not easy. What should I say to this man? What should he say?

There are many things to say. First, we must say that we are all sons and daughters of one Father, a Father who loves us and wants us to live as brothers. I must say that it is this Word which is the main challenge of the mission of the Church. It is a word of love and hope, but this speech continues to raise the ire of those who are unwilling to recognize that we are all brothers and sisters. When you look at the problems of today's world, the problems are all based on the refusal of man to accept the other as his brother: women in Afghanistan, the situation in the Holy Land between Jews and Palestinians, in Northern Ireland, the injustices in third world countries. However, we must proclaim the Word in all seasons and denounce evil, to rebuke and encourage. Faced with these difficult situations, the Church needs our spiritual and material support to continue its mission of evangelization. It needs prophets, missionaries, priests, not only able to proclaim the Word through great sentences, but also able to live and testify in setting a good example. For this, we must pray. We must pray because the devil wants to attack. The malicious one attacks the family by causing divisions among the spouses, siblings, children and parents and between friends. He even attacks the Church, sometimes using the priests or bishops and hinders sin until it combusts to scandal. Like Moses, we are encouraged to persevere in prayer to avoid falling into the traps of the devil, because God the master of the world never ceases to help us. It means we are called to reach out to others. We are also encouraged to be supportive of each other and above all to be in solidarity with other Christian communities scattered around the world. We must choose the path of unity; this exchange between different nationalities fosters the spread of teaching Christ to others. It means we need to be open to people outside of our culture, to witness, to hope and to enter into this universal dimension of the Church. Throughout the world there are thousands of people, seminarians, novices who are preparing to go on mission. The Church needs money to support them. It also needs money for the building of churches and seminaries, for the food and the academic preparation of these young men and women who answer the call of God to proclaim His word. This means that it is a responsibility of the community that concerns us all and each one of us, is invited to contribute to the success of this mission.

On one hand, mission means to go to another and share with him the word of God which is a word of faith, hope and love. On the other hand, mission does not only mean going to a foreign country. In a culture that wants to promote aggression, negativity, pride and even barbarism, we are invited to accept the responsibility to be missionary by going to our neighbors, the people who are also waiting for Christ. If you're a couple and find it difficult to communicate because it is one of you who still wants to control the other, try to question your selfishness and be ready to be open to the other's needs. If you live alone and you find that loneliness is heavy, try to think about what St. Teresa of Avila said, "Let nothing disturb you, nothing scare you, he who lives by God owns everything. God alone suffices".

We Need Wisdom To Be Faithful To The Faith

THE POWER OF GOD'S WORD is a force and an appeal to wisdom for a person to keep his faith in a world where people tend to live in a false social status and cultural prestige that ultimately lead to nothing. The point is that if man no longer differentiates between good and bad, this is the beginning of his decadence. Thus, we are now witnessing a crisis in the Catholic faith which is, in part, a crisis of values in an environment marred by easy living and comfort. We have to proclaim the gospel in a context marked by religious indifference and religious hostility. It's an indifference that claims to have no interest in what we call religious symbols, rituals, dogmas, church life etc. […]. But when a family member decides to no longer practice his faith, perhaps because of arrogance or for personal reasons or because he no longer believes the language of the Church, we must pray for him because, as Scripture tells us very well: "Indeed, you will be hated by all nations on my account. Many will falter then, betraying and hating one another. False prophets will rise in great numbers to mislead many. Because of the increase of evil, the love of most will grow cold. The man who holds out to the end, however, is the one who will see salvation (Mt. 24: 10-13)". It is a word of love inviting us to live our life in this world with great spiritual discernment and prudence in order not to engage in these mortal gods of doubt, indifference and wickedness. We must always remember that Christ became incarnated in our world to tell us exactly our origin, to remind us of our identity. We have been created as human beings in the likeness of God. To accept, to believe in God and worship Him, we

97

must be humble in admitting that without Him, we will perish. If we are too arrogant, too entrenched in the material wealth of this world, there will be no place for God in our lives. It is a commandment to worship the one true God and it is also a commandment to transmit to our children the true faith and to teach them the tradition of the promises made to Abraham and his descendants. The Church is a sign and sacrament of that promise that God has made. The Lord is there beside us. He does not reveal himself in outward signs where there are noisy and spectacular events but He works inside our hearts and never abandons us in distress. When persecution comes within your family, do not panic; we must turn to God because He himself is the strength of the witnesses, the martyrs and the suffering. We have nothing to fear from external events because our strength is in Him and He loves us. Since we live in a global village, we must put aside our prejudices to achieve good communication and contribute to world peace. We cannot talk about peace and continue to be aggressive in our language. This does not work. Peace begins with one person, two people, and it extends as you go. We must recognize the need for interpersonal relationships as a community and develop this spirit of interdependence to promote peace. If we as Christians do not recognize that there is something missing in our spiritual journey when we turn away from God, the entire world will suffer greatly. The reality is that, if I hurt someone, I am hurting myself and one day or another, I pay for it. But our problems come from the fact that it is easy to turn away from the main message of the Gospel and give to our body and soul all the illusions and false interpretations.

We must be sensitive to the suffering of others. The suffering of someone must be ours. If they torture someone in the world, one man, one woman, one black, one white, that suffering must be ours too. The spirit is everywhere and we can work together for the well being of the world. Thus, we must be positioned with all those working to change attitudes and behaviors for a better world. As long as your heart remains open to the needs and expectations of others, anything is possible. God can enter with His promises of happiness. Yes, faith is difficult when life is difficult. But several before us have been there. Thus, we must fight not to lose faith, because what good is falling into doubt if it is for us to lose our soul?

TODAY A SAVIOR IS BORN:
IT IS CHRIST THE LORD

FOR THE PAST TWO MILLENNIA, a scandal has occurred in our world: A child was born in a stable where some shepherds were guarding their flocks in the neighborhood. The heavenly messengers came to this opportunity to give a message indicating the nature and identity of this child. They said that the Savior is born. Since then, man has continued to protest and revolt against what they believe to be a blasphemous statement and belief. When we go to the history of our world, we discover that governments, states, republics, people of all languages and all nations have done everything to destroy the message that this child came to bring to humanity. The problem is that Christ is a being who disturbs. Already at birth, he disdained the consideration of wealth and all the material possessions of this world. With such a program of life, He will not have many friends. The evidence is glaring in our eyes particularly during the preparation for the feast of Christmas. The streets are crowded with people everywhere shopping while many churches remain empty. This shows us that Christmas is not primarily the opportunity to go shopping and buy gifts, or replace furniture and clothes. It is rather the time given to remind us of the urgency to prepare our hearts to love, to make a phone call to someone, to forgive and to reconcile with our enemies and ensure that nothing obscures the Eucharistic celebration wherever we attend Mass.

There are no adequate words that can describe the joy of Christmas. This is not a joy thundering through which we say: "Merry Christmas" to each other, but rather an internal disposition hosted by the heavenly voice that says: "I bring you great and happy news. The Savior is born! Go and see, you will find a baby lying in a manger". And now the angels sing this hymn: "Glory to God in the highest". Yes, such celebrations, these wishes, these gifts and the decorations that we have organized, prepared and shared during this Christmas must truly be for the glory of God. Otherwise, we will be disappointed if we have given much and in return we get nothing. If we are frustrated because some little details are not to our taste and not in harmony with our expectations; we are missing the essential point. How can we celebrate Christmas, the feast of joy and reconciliation if we are unable to reconcile with ourselves, with a member of our family or with another? If we do not listen to the voice from Heaven, the voice that brings the rules and principles of faith, our Christmas won't be meaningful. Jesus is born and he was not born just anywhere; He was born in a barn. This is done to teach us something big, something much needed in this world: Humility. We all need it. The nobility of heart that led the wise men to Jesus, we must do everything we can to acquire it. We are all invited to become noble people, ready to sacrifice our own interest in order to think of one another. The meaning of Christmas is this: God gives all men the chance to save their lives but he respects everyone's freedom. Thus, man is responsible for his fate: He can contribute to his damnation or to his salvation.

The joy of Christmas brings hope for everyone particularly those who are facing many challenges in their lives. We can sometimes be tempted to ask for a sign from God especially when we are going through tough and difficult moments in our lives. When we have no jobs and an apartment to pay, children to feed and when we have health problems, persecution with members of our family, children who practice no more, and despite our prayers, changes are slow to occur. At this point, look for the sign of the love of God not in the spectacular things but in this poor sign understood only by the humble believer: That of the Annunciation. It is with faith that we will pass through the most horrible situations of our lives without blaming God. Yes, we should never forget of the episode of the Annunciation. From this beginning of the Incarnation, is revealed the true face of God and His Messiah. Mary accepts everything in faith: "Behold the handmaid of the Lord, may it be done to me according to thy word". May Christmas be a time for us to renew our faith, to discover that God is always there with us, with the human race as we have seen it through His Incarnation.

We need to understand that without God we are lost. We must fight for not coming to this illusion that we can live without God. The sin of Adam and Eve was to cut their dependence on God, because before their fall, they were completely dependent on God. Is not that what some are trying to see in the world today: the desire for a society without God? Thus, the Christian life is a fight to the end: a fight against the illusions of this world, against the flesh, doubt and many tempting traps in which we find ourselves. It is also a struggle against discouragement and jealousies and family disputes. We are invited to ask the Lord for the courage to take the resolution not to spend Christmas without our reconciliation with those who cause us many problems: spouse, father, mother, stepmother, neighbors, cousin, etc.[...]. It is by taking the risk of spreading the love around us that we announce the Good News concerning Christ, and, by doing so, we can really celebrate Christmas.

MAN, AN IRREPRODUCIBLE AND IRREPLACEABLE BEING

IN NEW TESTAMENT THEOLOGY, THE aggregation of converts to Judaism had three rituals: circumcision, baptism and sacrifice. Circumcision in Judaism was of a truly universal significance: it was not a carnal sanction restricted only to descendants of Abraham but it was also the introduction into God's covenant with his people offered to all. It has a relationship with the contemporary Judaism of Christ, with its universal mission of salvation (Mt 23: 15). But to the circumcision, Judaism added for the converts the requirement of purification as a baptism. This baptism, because it was the only rite payable, gained in significance adding to the first meaning of the purification of inclusion in the community who belonged to self circumcision. The baptism of Jesus by John in the Jordan meant not only an incorporation to Judaism through circumcision but it was also the emergence of a new covenant stating that all the observances of the old law were outdated. What is interesting in all of this is that the Jewish thought sees circumcision as the mark of God upon man, it is a seal that reminds them that they belong to God (cf. 1Rm 4: 11). Paul will keep the idea in his theology of Christian initiation (2 Cor 1: 21-22; Ep 1: 13; 4: 30). What the Heavenly Father decides about Jesus at baptism by John in the Jordan River meets all the promises of the Covenant. In the Jordan, the Lord Jesus has drowned the old man and gave birth to the new being. Jesus, true God, only begotten Son and at the same time as man, is a real and complete Jew. Being circumcised, he is introduced by baptism in the eternal act of generation by which the Father communicates his only begotten Son the fullness of his father's life. And, later, he will offer himself in sacrifice by his blood on the Cross.

O Son of God, you have come to humbly submit yourself to the baptism of John the Baptist, and free your children here from the slavery of sin, give us all this new gift of humility so that we may act like a child of light.

At Jesus' baptism, the heavens opened. The Spirit, like a dove, rested upon him. The Father's voice was heard: "This is my beloved Son, in whom I put all my love". This baptism which already has a very strong moral orientation and is used to prepare the Kingdom of God is received through Jesus. But for him who had no need to receive it, that baptism is a powerful and glorious manifestation of his divine filiation. He was baptized to crush in the water the heads of the dragon, to bar the road to sin. His baptism is the glorious manifestation of divine filiation, the testimony that God Father gives him, the fullness of the Spirit which is given. This baptism is for the Baptizer the opportunity to announce explicitly that baptism is still to come with the divine Pneuma. It is He who will baptize with the Holy Spirit (Jn. 1: 33 cf. Mt. 3: 11). He is the Lamb of God who takes away the sin of the world (Jn. 1: 29). It means that the baptism of Jesus became the solemn act which manifests His divine splendor and reveals himself as the Savior in view of the coming kingdom of God. Indeed, it was He who, from now on will baptize every man who is filled with the Spirit. It is He whom we must listen to as the Son of God. He will baptize not only with water, but with the Holy Spirit and fire (Mat. 3: 11).

This baptism that Jesus himself had given under such extraordinary circumstances, as the apostolic preaching and the early Church continue to emphasize, as the ancient Christian liturgy which was celebrated early in the celebration of the "Epiphany". The purpose of the baptism of Jesus was not the Levitical purity which the water of the Jordan River could not provide. Its meaning was to erase sins. John does not welcome people in a new religious community. What He wants is to prepare the second coming of the Messiah and the Kingdom of God. It is to contemplate what any aspiring contemplative, every man of prayer attempts to obtain so that he may receive the mystery of God the Father, the Son and the Holy Spirit. John sees the Son, the eternal Word of God, and already recognizes the Savior. He hears the Father that nobody can see and the Father testifies that it is indeed His Son. He perceives the presence of the Spirit hovering over the waters, mother of all life (Gen. 1: 2). The Spirit descended on Mary at the Annunciation (Lk. 1: 35). This Spirit has come upon the apostles to fertilize their land and give eternal life. This Spirit gives us the strength to get through the difficulties and disappointments of life and makes us understand that we are not alone and that God is with us. We all need of this spirit that will provide the spiritual health that can make us identify the Lamb of God in all circumstances. As followers of Jesus, we will experience hard times, persecution, disease and even death. In fact, some of us will experience the cross of Christ in all its magnitude and if we do not have the spirit of God within us to give this force, there will be doubt and rebellion.

THE BEATITUDES

J ESUS PROCLAIMED THE BEATITUDES AT the beginning of his
apostolic ministry. He spoke to a crowd representing all ages, all nations
and all colors. These beatitudes can be read from different perspectives as
they were lived before Jesus by the prophets and the learned of all times.
They have been experienced by Jesus and Mary during their earthly life
and as Jesus calls all men to live them after him, with the help of the Holy
Spirit in the rest of the world's history and the Church. But what did Jesus
say to these people? In fact, He has presented and presents the eternal bliss
that may already be living on earth. He has given them and it gives us
the hope of the Kingdom. What is striking in the Beatitudes is that Jesus
does not offer an option. It shows the way, the only way to happiness. The
contents reveal not an earthly or material happiness that is fragile and
volatile, but the participation in the glory of God in Heaven who is inside
the virtue of hope. The message of the Beatitudes does not give time for
arrangements or preparation. The person who hears this message of the
Beatitudes does not negotiate them. He or she receives them or rejects
them. Often some scholars present the Beatitudes as something that is
opposed to the morality of the Ten Commandments. This opposition is
artificial. Both texts refer to two different sides of the same moral: that
man is called to recognize in every human being the image of God. The
Beatitudes are the expression of the promise of happiness made to those
who take the Ten Commandments seriously, and through them, seek to
answer the call of love of God. In today's world, Christian morality, with
a shade of contempt in the pronunciation is often understood as a series

of prohibitions opposed to a true liberation of man. We are witnessing the decline of morality in which people do not reflect the image they project or the testimony they give. They think they are free and have no accountability to anyone. But we must know that morality is never just a private matter. It concerns the body of Christ that we are. By this, Jesus calls us to do small acts of peace every day of our lives. It is too easy to say when we are angry: "It is I! That's the way I am, I cannot do otherwise".

We are invited through the Eucharist to taste the Beatitudes of Christ, to ask the Lord for His grace out of these isolated situations in which we find ourselves. Only with the grace of God through meditation, personal effort, prudence and the desire to be holy will we accept the Beatitudes. This is the path of poverty, gentleness, compassion, obedience, mercy, purity of heart and even of peace, persecution, patience. It is given to those who live in either one of the nine proposed routes encountered in the Beatitudes and which we must ask God to bless us with. We must absorb each one of them, and seek beyond the happiness on earth. It means to gain access to the true happiness offered to us, Jesus presents us in the Beatitudes the need to leave some circles, some networks and even some people who do not help us out of our slavery and our sins. These people may decide to persecute us if we decide to leave them to be faithful to God. They want to keep us in this earthly happiness while we are currently ourselves in isolation. This makes us suffer more. In this titanic struggle, which will intensify until the glorious return of Jesus and where each day the mystery of iniquity becomes apparent, Satan is more than ever the persecutor over the mystery of Jesus. He tries to assemble a coalition of falsehood and violence through which all men are deceived by the allurements of the world and are complicit in unjust structures. But he himself seeks to infiltrate into the households, the convents, the Christian communities, to try and destroy from within the Church of Jesus. If we pray and we frequent the Sacraments, we must watch with more attention and look forward to the most treacherous persecution. But let us not be afraid and do not forget that persecution is a blessing. When we are persecuted, despised, and we are still able to love, forgive and make peace, it is to us that the Beatitudes are addressed.

True Faith Requires Obedience

THE CHURCH INVITES US TO dare a new start to really make this encounter with Christ. It invites us to come out of the lies in which we live to follow Christ into another mountain which is the true initiation that we seek; it means the full revelation of the glory of God. Abraham is asked to abandon all his bearings, all his possessions, everything that belongs to him, without knowing the destination. Imagine the scenario: the Lord comes to you and asks you to leave your wife, your husband, your home, your family, your bank accounts, jewelry, your makeup, your dress, and what is worse, He charges you to leave your dog or cat, all things great and small and go somewhere that He will show you. Would you not freak out upon hearing this? What the Lord asks Abraham, he also asks us. He does not ask you to leave your home, your family, your husband or wife, and walk in the street despondent, but rather an existential transformation of yourself that He requests. Each of us is personally called by Christ on the mountain of revelation where He wants to unveil to us the mystery of his person and also show us a demonstration of the uncreated light to better prepare ourselves and to live the ordeal of the Cross that concerns us all.

Christ asks us all here today to take a little time to meet him on the mountain. He wants to reveal His light so that when trials, pain and difficulties occur, we may remind ourselves that He is there. That is what gives us the strength and desire to continue to advance in faith to His kingdom and never despair of God's loving plan. You know there are people who commit the mistake of giving up, stop praying and believing when they suffer the trials of illness or the death of a family member. But for people who agree to be transformed by this invitation, we understand that, when we have problems, it is our faith in the Lord that will give us the humility to seek, to talk to someone who can help us get out of it. Before being disfigured by the spit and the wickedness of men, the Lord Jesus was transfigured in glory to show his disciples the treasures of his eternal wisdom. The temptations we face in our lives can be understood and rebuked with the choice of Jesus at the threshold of his mission and we are able to behold his glory. For when we are subject to temptations, we are called to glory: the glory of the Word. Jesus never abandoned his goal, but he was buried in our flesh to go faithfully until the end of the human adventure. The Transfiguration scene gave us a prelude of this glory; the three apostles who devote themselves to the cause of the Lord testify. The experience is so strong and rewarding that Peter asked the Lord to make three tents. He wants to bask in the radiance of the glory of God to satisfy them. You see that even the natural desire of God was manipulated and Peter forgot that the characteristic of true love and the essence of holiness are to seek no glory than to be loved. Thus, in this selfish attitude of Peter, he received no reply to his query. Preferably, a cloud casts its shadow on the characters and now the vision is lost. Suddenly, the magisterial voice of the Father refers to Jesus' word: "Listen to Him". In our society today, these words of the Father cost a million words because among all the words that reach our ears, there are those of Jesus that we must listen. This word asks us to leave our worldly goods comprised of jealousy, envy, pride, arrogance and malice in response to the invitation of Jesus in the building of the new man, recreated by the omnipotent word of the Father.

All these actors in the words of Scripture are there to make us understand that we too are called to a similar glory. Already, it lies dormant in us because of our baptism, our confirmation and the Eucharist which is communion with the transfigured body of Jesus. But like Jesus, we must wait our time. The time has not yet come when we rise in our flesh, in the glory. We still have to live, suffer and die. However, we must accept everything not as we support a fatality, but as a total love to the Father.

HE TOLD ME EVERYTHING I'VE DONE

AFTER WE RECOVER FROM THE experience of transfiguration, we are invited to go to three catechumenal stations referring to water in three important chapters of the Gospel of John. The Samaritan woman and Jesus, tired, sits down at the well of Jacob, which still exists today. He asks for a drink from the woman, a Samaritan woman looking for love. It is in the atmosphere of this unexpected meeting that the Gospel of John brings the decisive words of Jesus to believers and especially to those who receive baptism at Easter night.

Jesus appears to all his followers as a source of living water. This water is the Spirit, the gospel is baptism. All are invited to drink free (Isaiah 55, 1). No one, regardless of how he has lived so far, is excluded. Just recognize who is the Messiah and who can really give us the happiness we all seek. This will give us faith in all circumstances of our daily life. Jesus offers us abundant water that flows from his pierced heart to give eternal life to the world. The source of living water for us is Jesus who will help us to grow and become new creatures. We heard the voice of the Lord invite us to drink this water, which is the Spirit, the Gospel and baptism. Jesus asks for a drink, and the surprise is that he gives something to drink to the woman. May this give us the Humbleness needed for us to walk in the newness of life, to recognize our weaknesses and without any shame present them to the Lord in order to receive His mercy. Lord, you told us, if we hear your voice, do not close our hearts; grant us to be always attentive to create this spirit of communion which we so desperately need in our Church and in our world.

An Event Absolutely Unique and Rationally Unprovable

THE RESURRECTION OF CHRIST REVEALS to all believers and to the whole world that God's Kingdom is already reflected in the death of Jesus. At the negative peak of the cross followed the positive peak of the resurrection. Thus, the conqueror of death that the Church celebrates on Easter day is Jesus, the man whom the apostles had seen, heard and followed on the roads of Galilee and Judea. In the Gospel accounts of the Resurrection, we are engaged primarily in an experience of identification: we recognized Him. Certainly, the Lord is now living in a brand new condition, but in depth the person has not changed. Thus, the true personality of Jesus can be understood in the light of Easter Sunday and Easter Sunday can reveal its true meaning only in the darkness of Good Friday. In other words, this means that the difficulties and problems we encounter in our lives have meaning only if we are associated with the suffering experienced by Christ during Friday on the road to Calvary. Alerted by Mary Magdalene, Peter and John, the eldest and the youngest of the apostles run to the tomb of Jesus. John who tells us the fact and Peter after entering the tomb saw and believed. Through their testimony and that of the first witnesses, we also believe that Jesus is alive; He is risen. It is not a doctrine, but He is someone, someone who is already there but will be revealed in the future. The resurrection of Christ says that we must get out of our graves in which we dwell with the purpose of choosing Jesus. It means to love, opt for the truth, the goodness and hope. This cannot be a matter of emotion or sentimentality, or popular piety. We cannot talk about what we do not know. If you're dealing with people who have never enjoyed life and never experienced the love of God, they will make your life miserable. Beware: the love that is evoked here is not about having a boyfriend or girlfriend, a husband, a wife or a mistress somewhere. The love spoken of at the resurrection is a love that asks us to leave our tombs of negativity, attachment, insecurity and selfishness to get to really love like Christ. If you're dealing with someone who is always negative, always criticizing, always crying about his fate and refuses to control his nerves and to undermine the respect of others, you will find it will take a lot of prayers to remain calm and turn the other cheek.

As parents and grandparents, we must constantly reflect on how we educate our children so that when they grow up, they may know how to endure all sufferings and wait in hope. We cannot grow emotionally as if we were sitting in a beautiful chair where we are served a delicious dinner daily on a silver platter. But when you've been raised in an environment where you have learned how to deal with situations of pain, you may be able to understand that it is not a curse or a punishment but a gift for a specific purpose.

Yes, the resurrection of Jesus requires that we break with all customs and cultural traditions which have no connection with our personal lives. For example, we may be so used to getting worried for anything that it becomes a second nature. We can finish celebrating the Eucharist, and even before we reach our car, we cannot even wait an hour, we have to light a cigarette while having said: "I received the living God and my heart is full of joy". What does this mean? It is so easy for us to be slaves of our passions; why are we unable to be slaves of the love of God? The resurrection of Christ tells us that the cross is not the last word on Jesus, because God will rise Him from the dead. The cross surmounts the scandalous nature into something positive for everyone. It is in this sense that the resurrection of Christ invites us to hope. Thus, it is important to ask ourselves how we approach this basic event, the capital point of our faith. The fact of the resurrection is exceptional and unique in its kind. It is an act of faith despite the evidence. It is a fact that has been lived, however it has not been photographed by cameramen. It is primarily a meeting with Christ who communicates to us and gradually transforms our lives, our existence as men into a life that is new, and as children of God. This is our Christian faith.

WHY CONTINUE TO CRY OVER OUR FATE?

THERE IS A WHOLENESS THAT awaits us once we begin to follow Jesus. It rests on the fact that faith always refers to Jesus, someone real and unique, situated in history and not an idea. This Jesus of Nazareth who since birth has experienced poverty, threats, persecution, exile and so on is recognized as Christ and Lord. The resurrection has become that of one who lived, performed miracles in Galilee and Judea, who died on the cross but who, before death, delivered himself into the hands of the Father. It is the resurrection of a particular man, very special, the Son of the Father. It is the resurrection of the One who suffered for us and showed us the path that we should walk in his footsteps. Thus, we have every reason not to continue to cry over our fate and fall into despair or suicide but to live our lives with patience, endurance and total abandonment to the Father. This means that for inner peace, we must decide to seek and find Jesus in the multiple difficulties of our daily lives. By dying on the cross and rising from the dead, Christ showed us the way of life. Light and salvation of all peoples, send into our hearts the fire of Your Spirit so that as priests, teachers, conscientious lawmakers, national leaders, wise parents, we may have cheerful hearts to serve you in one another and so, respond to our vocation. We pray to you Lord. Help us to renounce everything that hinders us from a life of holiness, all that prevents us the desire to grow with you.

THE LORD CALLS US
EACH BY NAME

THE LORD KNOWS US BETTER than ourselves and we have such value in His eyes that He will be in front of us when danger threatens us, giving us strength through His Body and Blood. He will fight without fear of injury or hatred wherever we are threatened. In the parable of the Good Shepherd, Jesus develops two important themes especially: that of the door and the voice. To enter the kingdom, one must agree to hear the call and enter. However, there is a door. Jesus himself is the door, and he defines himself as the only door to enter His Kingdom. He is also the one who holds the keys to the door. He opens it. No one can close it. More than any other, the Good Shepherd is an image of Easter. We must give our lives to God in the same way Jesus did. In other terms, we must surrender to Him if we want to live in peace and reach happiness. When a shepherd is good, He gives his life to save his flock. That is what Jesus did. It is true that He risks His life. However, He knows that the Father ordered him to finish the fight because He will win in the end. Even death which is the last enemy; this enemy will be defeated eventually. Along the same way, as parents in a household, we must be willing to sacrifice our life for the welfare of our children so they may grow in a normal environment, with a father and a mother.

The Lord continues to call us so that we may walk with Him into the spirit of giving and offering either as parents or as celibate faithful. Each of us is called personally and must meet the Lord when our name is called, like Simon or, better still, like Mary Magdalene who recognizes

Jesus' voice. The relationship that the Lord has with each one of us is an affectionate relationship. Each is recognized for himself. These are things that cannot be formulated: it is impossible to describe the tone of voice. But anyone who has heard the voice will always recognize it. In this victory, the Good Shepherd leads his flock. He opens the door for the sheep. Now they can come and have life in abundance. This is the reason why the resurrection of Christ guarantees our own resurrection as the fate of the herd is linked to the fate of the Good shepherd. Not only do they know and recognize His voice, but because he is the Pastor, there are also those who want to follow Him. As the Good Shepherd, Jesus announces how terrible the battle is and that He is coming to our rescue. He will not come just for a visit but He has come to adopt us; we are his dearest possession. The image of a sheep is very important to understand the depth of love Jesus has for us, because the sheep is an animal which is extremely vulnerable and so constantly threatened. More than others, it needs to be guarded and protected. Also, as a couple, your love needs to be protected and renewed. If after 30, 40 or more years in a relationship, you discover that because of some of your habits, you can no longer accept one another and that you are constantly in dispute to the point that married life has no meaning, well, I'll tell you this, if you don't marinate your marriage with the spices of love, patience, and respect, it will be a cold relationship that has no flavor. Unfortunately, this is what happens to many couples: they have stopped being lovers, being nice and tolerant and they no longer find charm in the presence of the other. If you see that your marriage is running out of flavor, it's time to leave the bad habits; they are no longer useful. It is also time to go and replenish the spice for a good meal. But where do you buy the ingredients for your love to have good flavor? You should go to the event of the resurrection of the Lord and that is where the Good Shepherd tells you how. Nothing can separate us from the love of God, nothing but our own will to get rid of Him. This insurance based on the word of Christ is the source of all Christian courage. That is far from being a presumption. It is trust. The tenacity, the patience and the strength of the martyrs give us new purpose in our spiritual journey to remain faithful and not to give up.

GOD WANTS TO BRING US
TOGETHER THROUGH HIS CHURCH

PENTECOST IS THE SIGN OF the advent of salvation history. Compared to the sign of the devil which is a magic sign of fascination and wonder and division, the intervention of God through Pentecost is a sign of grace and communion in the life of the Church beginning with the apostles. Therefore, they could understand, communicate and express themselves through a common language. It is a sign of the closeness of the kingdom of God and a sign of the negation of the kingdom of Satan. It is the decline of all satanic forces, all that paralyzes, alienates and enslaves man. Pentecost is a sign of the security of Hope in the newness that is unheard of. The Holy Spirit on the day of Pentecost is manifested as a strong wind, as a new presence that bridges and strengthens as a fire which burns and gives witness with confidence to the risen Christ. The event of Pentecost is the fulfillment of prophecy of the Old Testament. It is meant to free the apostles from their chains so that they learn how to build unity in the bond of the Holy Spirit. But in our daily lives, what does all this mean? How, as human beings, can we take advantage of the fruits of the Pentecost? As believers living in the world, we are invited to open ourselves to this event which asks us to be with God. We are invited to receive the graces that God sends into our lives. But it is imperative that we agree on the words because if we do not understand the word grace in the theological meaning of the term, we will be disappointed. Grace is a supernatural force that is given to man to help him live a better life, a life that goes beyond human dimensions. We are called to overcome our status as creatures to return to God in a relationship like that of father and son. Thus, God does not reserve it to select people rather He gives it to everyone.

We are invited now to live the life of Christ and be a mirror in which others see that together we destroy the walls that exist between us. With Pentecost, it is the beginning of a Church rich not in money but in love: everyone puts into practice his talent for the good of others. The Spirit unites the diversity and builds the Church. To get to live this spirit of unity, we must fight against the vices that block communication between us. For example, it is sad to see how the family is now contested by many satanic forces. People who are married to express their love to one another must fight every day against the interference of the devil which will occur in everyday things, sometimes very simple. When we see people who can no longer accept each other because they can no longer control their nerves toward one another; we must pray to the Holy Spirit in order to become aware of the situation and make changes to their behavior. Without it there will be no improvement. To live in love with each other on a daily basis, it is the product of grace and human effort. The Holy Spirit will give us good ideas for communication. It is very easy to fall into conflict. However, we all can learn and live in the radiance of the manifestation of the Holy Spirit for the common good.

FAITH AND ACTION GO TOGETHER

THIS MESSAGE COMES TO SHOW us the importance of justice, charity and hope in our spiritual journey. There is a very close relation between faith and the gestures which we pose in our relationship with one another. We cannot really love God if we do not like our neighbor, but the problem that we all confront as human beings is that we have difficulty in identifying our neighbors. Who is my neighbor? This is the fundamental question which each liturgy raises to us. Is my neighbor the one who thinks like me or who has the same material possessions as me? Do I practice justice where I work, do I contribute to the happiness of others or do I sow division because of my selfishness and my imprudence? It is necessary to think of these superficial relationships where sometimes you think you have a friend: in front of you hands you a smile, but behind lashes a knife in your back. This kind of defect cannot build harmony and confidence in a relationship, whether it is within a friendship, a marriage, a family or a community. When there is no trust and sincerity in a relationship, love cannot last very long. Sometimes you may be sincere and open yourself while the other person is acting like a spy to record every word and gesture you do so that later he or she can use them viciously against you. As Christians, it is necessary to request from the Lord the grace of the Holy Spirit to avoid this practice which destroys the peace that He came to offer us. That is the reason why Jesus said that we cannot serve God and Mammon. The worst thing which can happen to us, is to be content with our own performance of life, not to have anything to reproach us, to be stagnant without any growth. To enter the intimacy of the heart of

Jesus, it is necessary for us to be recognized as sinners, humble sinners who count only on the mercy of God and not on their own forces. Thus, the requirement of reconciliation and Mass go hand in hand with the purpose of acquiring humility. To be humble is to recognize our limits and to let God enter our lives to cure us, to give us the force and courage in difficult moments. This is where faith is important; it will help us live through these moments. It will take humility from our part to turn to the Lord. To be humble is to surrender to God; it is also to look at each one of our brothers with a glance of tenderness; this glance that God employs for the most lost of his children. The Lord holds a love and a tenderness, a readyness to die for them. We witness this love and humility from our Savior and from this encounter we are converted. To be humble is this conversion of love and humility in this encounter with our Savior. When we reach this spiritual maturity, this stage of life in which we let God become the Master of our life, we will no longer need to be egotistical. It is a message that concerns us all, an upsetting message inviting us to prayer, an awakening to our weaknesses. It is a question of presenting these weaknesses to the Lord for whom nothing is impossible. It is not a question to say: "This is how I am; I cannot change". Solidarity to one another, with tenderness and gentleness is the road for the future and success. We cannot be Christians who are locked up in their boxes any more, forgetting the misfortune of the others. It is necessary to be open, to learn from others particularly those who preceded us and those who are still alive. We have also to pray for those who persecute us and those who have wounded us. We must also pray for those who are not nice and patient toward us. If you have a husband or a wife who has no patience and who does not want to take time to communicate and is irritated for nothing, pray for him/her. Through the message of St Paul, the Church wants to point out to us the power of prayer. Jesus wants that we be perfect like our Father! How is this possible? Jesus who knows the heart of the Father attaches such an importance to brotherly love; it is a sacrifice of our pride to leave our offering in front of the altar to go to reconcile us with our brother. He says all that to us because He wants us to be happy. The Happiness that He promises to us is not in wordly goods, nor in power, nor in the titles we hold, nor in glory and jealousy, nor in the selfishness that corrode the heart. Happiness is found in doing the will of God.

KEEP THE FAITH OF THE LORD IN OUR LIVES

THERE ARE MANY PROBLEMS IN the world of today: misery, unemployment, dictatorships, injustices, abuses, secularism. More and more, we witness a rise of nationalism, fanaticism and extremism obliging some followers to become cruel, indifferent and intolerant. In addition, we live in a world where there exists a culture that wants peace but deaf to the cries of the poor, a culture that wants justice but leans to dictatorships and totalitarian systems to reach its goal. In addition, the tendency toward socialism and communism approaches to resolve these problems is slowly making its appearance in many western governments. The scary thing is that mistrust and division between social classes and, the sharing of wealth are encouraged by leaders whose only aim is to present themselves as the only ones who care about the poor so that they can remain in power and control the people. It means that man is a being capable of anything. He is a being who can do everything in the field of love and in the field of hatred even though this being claims to serve God. It does not matter the social class to which those people belong. It is important for him to turn to God in order to know how to live and behave. We all have the same Father, a Father who loves us and who wants that we live like brothers. It is this Word which constitutes the deciding point of the mission of the Church. The force of the Gospel and of the Eucharist is a force of reversal of the hearts and a call to wisdom for a person to maintain his faith in a world where one tends to live in pride, false social and cultural prestige which finally leads to nothing, but as long as man does not make the difference between good and evil, he will be lost. Thus, we experience today a crisis in the Catholic faith which is a crisis of the values in a society spoiled by a life of comfort. We have to announce the Gospel to a society marked by the religious indifference, and it is to these men and women marked more or less by this indifference that it is necessary to bring the good news. It is an indifference which claims not to have any interest with what one calls religion, the religious symbols, the rites, the dogmas, the life connected with the church. But, when a member of your family decides not to practice his faith anymore, perhaps out of arrogance, or for personal reasons or because he does not believe any more in the language of the Church, it is necessary to pray for him, because as the prophet Malachi reports it in the Scriptures: "The day is coming now, burning like a furnace and all the arrogant and evildoers will be like stubble. The day that is coming is going to burn them up, says the Lord Sabbaoth, leaving them neither root nor stalk. But for you who fear my name, the sun of righteousness will shine out with healing in its rays" (Mal. 4: 1-2). It is a word of love inviting us to look at this world here with spiritual understanding and prudence not to devote ourselves to these mortal gods of doubt, indifference and wickedness. It always should be remembered that Christ incarnated himself in our world to tell us our true origin, to point out our identity to us. To believe in a God and to adore Him, it is necessary to be humble by admitting that without Him, we will perish. If we are too proud, too sure of material wealth of this world, there will be no more place for God in our life. It is a command to adore only one true God and it is also a command to transmit to our children this faith and to ensure their future in inculcating in them the tradition of the promise made to Abraham and his descendants. The Church is the sign and the sacrament of this promise that God has made to us. The Gospel, with its ways, speaks to us about the end of time. But the Lord is there, close to us. He does not appear in external signs noisy and spectacular, but He smolders in each one of us and never gives up in our distress. When persecution comes inside your family, one should not panic; it is necessary to turn to God, because He himself is the force of the witnesses, the martyrs and the suffering ones. We have nothing to fear because our strength is in Him and He loves us. In addition, we must put aside our prejudices to arrive at a good communication and thus to contribute to world peace. We cannot speak about peace and continue to be aggressive. That does not go together. Peace starts with a person, two people and that extends progressively. We must recognize this need for interpersonal relationships as a community and develop this spirit of interdependence to promote peace. We sometimes however do not recognize that; our spiritual growth is then stymied. If I behave badly with somebody, I will do harm to myself, and one day or another, I will pay for it. But our problems come from not harmonizing our body and conscience. If I refuse to listen to my conscience then I may be subject to several mistakes in my life because our conscience is the place where God talks to us so that we remain always in the truth.

THE NECESSITY OF AN
ENCOUNTER WITH THE LORD

WE ARE INVITED TO EMBARK on a new departure with the purpose of making this encounter with the Lord. He invites us to leave the lies in which we are firmly settled to follow Him towards another mountain where the true encounter we seek, the full revelation of the glory of God must take place. Abraham is invited to give up all his reference marks, all his possessions and all that belongs to him, without knowing the destination of the voyage. Imagine yourself in the following scenario: the Lord comes towards you and asks you to give up your wife or husband, your house, your family, your bank accounts, your jewels, your make-up, your dresses and what's worse, He asks you to give up your dog or your cat and to go to a place that He will show you. What the Lord requested from Abraham, He also requires of us. However, it is important to understand the content of this message. The Lord does not ask you to give up your house, your family, your husband or wife, and to live in the street like a destitute person; it is rather an existential transformation of your person that He asks of you. Each one of us is personally convened by Christ on the mountain of the Revelation where he wants to reveal to us the mystery of His Person, and also to show us a manifestation of the light to better prepare us for the terrible test of the Cross which concerns us all. Christ asks us all to take a little time to meet Him on the mountain. It is there that He wants to reveal to us His light, so that at the time of the tests, the pain and the difficulties we may experience His presence. It is exactly that encounter which will give us the force and the desire to continue to advance in the faith towards His Kingdom and never despair or question His presence or love. There are people who capitulate and stop praying when they undergo tests of disease, death of a member of their family. But, for people who agree to change their heart by this invitation that Christ makes to us, we will understand that when we have problems, it is our faith in the Lord which will give us humility to seek Him, to speak to Him and to listen to Him.

WE MUST KNOW HOW TO WAIT

L IKE JESUS, WE MUST WAIT our hour. The hour has not come yet
when we will be glorified in our flesh. It is necessary for us to know
how to live, and suffer, and die. Not as one who supports a fate, but in a
total love of the Father, in a constant attitude of obedience like Jesus, with
the certainty of our confidence in Him. We are invited to drink in the
same way as the Samaritan woman, whose life was troubled. It is in the
atmosphere of this unexpected meeting that the Gospel of John locates the
decisive words of Jesus for the believers and in particular for those who
will receive baptism on the night of Easter. Jesus presents himself to the
catechumens as the living water. This water, it is the Spirit, it is the Gospel,
it is the baptism. All are invited to come to drink. No one is excluded.
With such an invitation, it is enough to recognize that Jesus is the Messiah
who can really give us the happiness we all are looking for. In abundance,
Jesus delivers to us this water which runs from His transpierced heart to
give to the world eternal life. By drinking this water, we are able to renew
ourselves. We heard the voice of the Lord who invited us to drink this
water. Let us address our prayers to Him so that we may recognize our
weaknesses and without any shame to present them to the Lord in order
to receive his forgiveness.

THE RESURRECTION CALLS
US TO AN ENGAGED LIFE

THE EVANGELIC ACCOUNTS OF THE Resurrection put us in front of a whole experience of identification: We recognized it. Admittedly, the Lord lives from now on but under a very new condition. However, in-depth, the person did not change. Thus, Good Friday is understood only in the light of Easter Sunday and the Easter Day reveals its true direction only in darkness of Good Friday. The resurrection of Christ comes to say to us that it is important to bring peace to people living around us and this implies a lot of efforts on all sides. To reach this level of peace, it is important that we nourish us with His Eucharist. It is there that we will find the security and the true happiness that we seek. Each time we receive communions, the Lord seals with us an always new eternal alliance in what it operates in our wounded hearts. Let us ask him to help us to build the unity necessary in our personal lives. The Lord invites us to be bread of life for the world: For those who live in loneliness or without hope, or the victims of abuses of all kinds. For us here present, it is important for us to pray so that Jesus the Lord continues to feed us with His Body and Blood and to be the strength of our life.

THE WORD OF GOD, SOURCE OF OUR STRENGTH

WE ARE INVITED TO PROCLAIM the word of God to the whole world. Sometimes, it is a word that disturbs and those who proclaim it are sometimes exposed to the hostility of those who feel attacked as it was the case of Jeremiah. Following Jesus, the disciples revive, in their own way, the same tragic destiny. It was thus in the first years of the Church and the same applies today. The Good news is always the center of challenges. It is however not only the missionaries or the priests who are victims of the hostility of the others. For parents who already have adult children who do not practice the faith anymore, it is important to point out to them the urgency for them to reconcile themselves with God and his Church. It is not always easy. Such a move creates conflicts and because of that, sometimes you have children who do not speak with their parents any more. Thus, the good news often falls on unwilling ears. The Lord says to us not to be afraid and not to fear anything. The fact that the message is badly received is not a reason to conceal it. We must speak without being afraid of people because to speak for the Lord, is also a way to bring to these people the revelation of the mysteries of the Kingdom. In front of this opposition, Jeremiah entrusts his cause to the Lord and proclaims his conviction that God is with him. The Lord is our strength, our shield, our rampart, our refuge. Thus, we should not be afraid. The Lord also invites us to have confidence and faith in difficult moments. These words are addressed to the young people as well as with the elderly. Young people who cannot find work should not be afraid; they need to practice a little patience. You who begin a household should live without fear. Be not disappointed; it is normal that the beginning be difficult. For you who accept old age with difficulty, you who live alone and who are rejected: be without fear, be not afraid and with the help of prayer, uproot this force which paralyses you and separates you from the Lord. Today, in our society, many men and women undermine the Christian faith. People who are victims of these lifestyles, think that they find happiness and freedom in a rebellious attitude against anything that is spiritual. But isn't this the real risk to see their faith imprisoned by an environment which tends to cause them pain? The reality is that there are problems we may experience in our lives that no human being on earth can resolve nor can understand; only God can cure it. When a person is exposed to such a difficulty, where will he find the strength to get through it? It is not logical for a person to reject the faith or to claim to be an atheist. Such a form of seduction can kill the heart without attacking the body. The evil spirit which was opposed to our martyrs, with our prophets is still at work. With other means, it continues to seek to divert faith. But, do not let him confuse you. In a world that offers man so much possibility of true freedom and blooming, that made immense progress to the service of man, you are invited to free yourself from these idols that cannot truly satisfy the desires of the heart. It is by releasing yourself from these idols of the world that you will know true happiness. It is necessary to pray, it is necessary to make personal efforts, it is necessary to ask the Lord for His grace. If you are unmarried or widowed, do not be afraid to be alone. It is better to be alone than to be constantly in bad company, especially in the presence of people who do not help you live your Christian duties. If you always need the company of another person, do not be afraid to go and offer your help or your service in hospitals, in nursing homes or in places where people need you. Do not be afraid to be holy. Do not be afraid to discover your true vocation to collaborate in the expansion of this kingdom of truth and life. Such is the freedom with which Christ released us. It is not the freedom we've been promised through the illusions, the frauds and the powers of this world. Do not be afraid to call upon the Holy Spirit. It is He who will give us the strength to change and to be better people capable to love ourselves through the Lord instead of looking to people to love us.

The Church Is
Particularly Sensitive To
Discriminatory Attitude

THE HOLY FATHER ENTRUSTED TO all the dioceses the responsibility to contribute to inform and stimulate the consciences on this capital stake: the reciprocal respect of the ethnicities. Thus, each parish must be a place of reception and integration from abroad. We are also invited, like members of each parish in the Catholic Church, to widen the horizons of our cultures and our mentalities according to the dictates of Christ, in order to live the bond of unity that binds us. According to the book of Leviticus (Lv. 25, 23) we all are from abroad. We all carry within our blood a stain of immigrants. When we start forgetting that reality we become intolerant toward those who are taking their chances. The Lord reminds us that the ground belongs to me and you are for me only foreigners and hosts. Moreover this new conviction is extended to all the Disciples of Christ: since they are citizens of the celestial fatherland and fellow-citizens of the saints, they do not have a permanent residence here on earth. They live like nomads, always with their quest for the final goal. This biblical advice is intended to help us to give up any nationalist conceit and to be withdrawn from the narrow ideological blinders which create prejudices and walls between people and nations. In addition, it invites us to make constant efforts to release us from this cultural heaviness which inhibits sincere fraternity and hospitality. When this force of cohesion for charity does not exist in our relationship with one another, the ethnic and cultural differences become a source of division and dispersion. For the Christian, any human is the neighbor that he must love. He does not wonder about those whom he must love because, to wonder "who is my neighbor?" is already a way to set limits and conditions. Catholicism does not appear only by the fraternal communion of baptized, but it is also expressed by the hospitality which one gives abroad. The Catholic faith encourages the faithful to always welcome others; it is part of its religious membership. The faithful is to be committed to the refusal of any exclusion or racial discrimination and open to the recognition of the personal dignity of each one. The parishes have to be visible points of reference, easily identifiable and accessible, and they also have to be a sign of hope and fraternity in the middle of the social tensions and the explosions of violence that spread around the world. The listening of the same word of God, the celebration of the same liturgies, the fidelity to the same religious tradition can help us to overcome the prejudices which sometimes enter our minds.

The racist ideologies and behaviors which we are witnessing in the world of today take their roots in the reality of sin since the origins of humanity through the accounts of Cain and Abel. Even after 2000 years of evangelization, racism, division, and wickedness have not disappeared. There are alarming resurgences which arise in various spontaneous forms, officially tolerated or institutionalized. But Christ informs us solemnly: we will be judged on the attitude that we will have had towards the foreigner or towards the poor. There is a radicality that is present in the vocation of those who want to follow Jesus. This radical request shocks us. Who takes this way must know at the beginning that he will be the disciple of the marginalized: of a poor man with no place to put his head, of a man who has to take up his cross and once engaged in his mission, should not look behind. However, this stance disturbs the evil which seeks only to control us. One is too easily accustomed to see "Cafeteria Catholics" taking some and leaving some in the evangelic message. It is necessary to renew our baptismal engagement by receiving continuously the hard words of Jesus and to agree courageously to be disciples who walk in his footsteps, sure to find, across the stony way, the happiness of the true life.

JESUS, A KING WHO SHARES OUR SUFFERINGS

CATHOLICS OF ALL PARISHES AROUND the world are invited to meditate on Jesus who is presented in the Liturgy as the King of the universe. This meditation is important for our faith because it allows us to amend things that need to be amended in our lives particularly in our relationship with God and with our brothers and sisters. Jesus Christ is the King of kings who was born in a manger and who accepted to die on the cross to show us how to love and also to show us the way that leads to salvation. Jesus is King but He preferred to live a humble lifestyle among the poor in spirit contrary to the kings living in this world separated from the rest of the people. It might be difficult for us to comprehend all of this however; it is a powerful message for our spiritual growth where most people tend to see material possessions as a blessing to them and their family. The Kingdom of Jesus offers to us the possibility to live in this world with contentment and peace even though we may not have a lot of wealth. As believers, nothing disturbs us because we are never alone in our pains. The Lord is always there to support us. However, we must understand that every human person on earth has a cross to carry. Every father or mother converses with the Lord for something that is not going well in the family. A person may have all the wealth of the earth however; this does not mean that he or she is exempt of pains and problems in his or her life. There are many kinds of trials and hardships for a human person. They are situated at different levels and that is why it is essential that we turn to the Lord to receive the strength that will encourage us to keep going. Whenever we have problems in our lives, we must walk with the Lord in order to be protected. We must rely on Him for everything concerning our present and our future. If we do not look for the Lord and His help, we may have already been wired in many problems and then instead of resolving them or trying to get out of them to have a better life, we put ourselves in situations that bring more problems to us. We should not do that, because we have to love ourselves and do our best to eliminate problems in our lives. The enigma is the following: if we don't love ourselves and if we don't know how to treat ourselves properly, how can we expect to love another person? If we mistreat ourselves, we won't know how to bring love to others. Many people have forgotten that they must learn first how to love themselves but they rely on someone else to love them. When we are involved in a relationship looking for someone to love us, this relationship won't last very long. You can only maintain love through love. Is this not one of our many dilemmas in this world of today? Jesus as King knew how to find strength to move forward: In everything that was happening to Him, He always said to the Father: Thy will be done. He knew how to endure all kinds of hardships, he knew how to be patient and slow to anger. He did not blame God His father for what was happening to Him. He did not stop talking to God for His misfortune. In this way, He acted as a true Son. He is the King because no one else has ever done this before. Christ has done us a great service by showing us another way to deal with sufferings. On the cross, He surrendered himself totally to God, His Father, and that is what we are called to do: to have a lot of respect for God, to call upon Him and to put everything into His hands whenever we are experiencing any kind of difficulties. May our eyes be opened to the Light revealed by the King so that in the midst of the tragedies and challenges present in our lives we conform our thoughts and our sentiments to the humility of Christ.

We Can All Become A Messenger Of Love And Peace

W<small>E ARE ALMOST AT THE</small> end of the year and as a way for us to evaluate our own relationship with God and with one another, the Church gives us this season of blessing which is the Christmas season to reflect more about our last day here on earth. How will we be? Will we be in the grace of God? Do we have enough knowledge and spiritual maturity to maintain our faith until the end? Are we open to know more about our Catholic faith presented to us in the book of Catechism of the Catholic Church or do we remain Catholics only with the information we received when we made our first communion and confirmation? If that is the case, how can we defend it when we are attacked by extremists from other religions who try to intimidate us by reciting many verses from the Bible? This time of the year is a time of cleansing and purification to receive the Lord in our heart and to celebrate His coming in the world. We are more than ever reminded about the presence of Jesus among us. He came to show us how to love, how to forgive, and how to have confidence in God the father. He came to show us how to turn to the Lord in order for us to receive the strength to carry the crosses present in our lives. He came to teach us humility in terms of attitude: if we are not going to learn more on the Catholic faith, at least with an attitude of humility, trust what the Magisterium is saying regarding the position we should have on many subjects regarding the faith. Indeed the Lord will give us a better life where there will be no more pain and no more sufferings. The Lord will come back to introduce us to God His father so that we may share

His friendship and be part of the family. Because of the importance of this season in our faith, the liturgy puts more emphasis on the obligation we have to prepare our hearts and to welcome the Lord whose birthday we celebrate at Christmas. This is a time in which we all have the opportunity to improve not only our relationship with God but also our relationships with one another. This is the time to start anew and to decide to stay away from anything that is not bringing peace. As sinners, we are subjected to all kinds of temptations but with the help of the Lord present in our midst, we should not be afraid. The food we receive from the Lord is so powerful that we can become strong to face the challenges of life. For example, we don't always live in charity with one another and we don't always show care, respect and concern to those around us. Many times, we are very friendly outside, busy talking on the phone, sending messages to people we consider important in our lives while we tend to be difficult with the ones who are close to us. In our spiritual journey, the Catholic Church reminds us how important it is for us not only to pray for peace in the world but also to change our attitudes so that we may be an instrument of peace to everyone we meet.

PREPARE A WAY FOR THE LORD

I T IS TRUE THAT THE strength of our faith allows us to surrender to God in all the moments of hardship that we may experience in our lives. It is not something easy to do. To finally make the decision allowing the Lord to be the boss of your life will require a lot of prayer and common sense. There is no need for us to spend our entire life trying to be the controller in everything. No one is perfect in this world. In a relationship, if the other person can make a mistake, we too can be mistaken because we are all mortals. We must realize that this is the way to go and to experience happiness in our lives. Indeed, if we want peace inside the house, we need to make some sacrifices. We cannot have everything. Civil society may tell us that we are free to express ourselves anytime and anywhere. However, if we want to nurture peace and love with a spouse or with whomever we are sharing a relationship, we must know how to shut our mouth and present the other cheek. Otherwise, there will never be peace because two bulldozer types of temperament cannot live in the same house. That is the path everyone needs to go through in order to have peace with God, with the other person and with ourselves. The Lord Jesus knew it. This is the reason why he came to show us the way. If we follow the other path where we don't want to control our tongue we will always be miserable. To leave the relationship is not the solution because our bad habit will follow us wherever we go, unless we decide to change. Of course, the Lord loves us all. Many times, He gives us many blessings in our lives, but because of our behavior, the gift the Lord has given can be easily lost. We can contribute to its destruction and then later complain that God does not care about us. If the way we communicate or relate to people causes more anger and frustration, something needs to be done because the conflict is causing pain not only to the other person but also to us. All the minutes, hours, days and weeks we spend being in a bad mood, not willing to reconcile, is wasted time that is gone forever. The strength of our faith convinces us to believe that the Lord loves us all even with our weaknesses and with our fears. However, the same Lord who welcomes us without any guile is also calling us not to remain in our mediocrity and not to remain in our box. He is inviting us to move forward. This is where He is waiting for us to bring us the bliss that we are looking for. This is the time to clean up our behavior and to adopt habits that are connected more to civility, love and peace for our neighbor and also for us. If you receive a gift from the Lord, do your best to keep it alive and to take care of it.

The Encounter With The Lord Brings Joy To The Heart

EVEN THOUGH THERE ARE SOME people who are naturally joyful, it is not very common to meet a person who is at the same time: joyful, peppy and generous these days. We all have been challenged by situations of life and sometimes they have left within us some scars of sadness which impede us to relax and even to laugh. Some of us would be merry only under the influence of alcohol, otherwise we are lukewarm and not really in the mood of expressing something that is friendly. However, the Church constantly invites us to learn how to smile and be happy in every single activity of our daily life. You don't need to have a lot of things in order to be happy. Just the fact to be alive can be enough reason for us to always have a smile on our face. By having a smiling face, we can bring hope and peace to other people who are stressed out or sad. Nevertheless, to be happy is a decision that every person needs to make in his life no matter if the person is rich or poor. Who can give us happiness: a man, a woman, a friend, a lot of money? While all of them are good things to have in our lives, only in the Lord can man find a lasting and a true happiness. Pessimistic people will say that there is no happiness in this world. They only see misery, hunger and violence. The hedonistic ones will see happiness only in pleasures, drugs, alcohol, sex and material possessions. In this confusion, people will divorce 5 or 6 times searching for the perfect person. The truth is when you are trapped in this kind of cycle, the emptiness that it left in you will force you to look for more. But the answer for all of us who want to be happy is this: If you want to be happy, look for God. He is the only

136

one who will love you without any hypocrisy and who will love you with all your weaknesses and your bad habits. Even though you may meet a person who loves you, that person can continue loving you only if he remains in the Lord who is the source of all love. As a human person, we will not always do things in the proper way; that person will have to learn how to forgive you. If not, that love can disappear in a second. So, the happiness the Lord offers us is trust, confidence and abandonment to His will. If we act daily doing the will of God, we cannot be miserable. The Lord is the only one who can give us joy in good times to celebrate with others and strength in times of trials not to fall into despair.

THE MANIFESTATION OF THE LORD, A BLESSING TO THE WORLD

FOR THOSE WHO CAN REALLY understand the meaning of God's coming in our world, they have a lot to be thankful for. The Christmas season reveals in evidence the love of God for us and also the many blessings we receive with the presence of Jesus in our world. Not only has He brought peace to all nations on Earth but He has also brought to humanity the gift of forgiveness. Through Him, our sins can be forgiven and we can also forgive those who do us wrong. Now that the Lord is being presented to the whole world, it means that the world is no longer under the control of evil. Darkness does not have the last word because the Lord God has revealed His presence through Jesus Christ who reigns in our life now and forever. For us, Christians it is an enormous blessing. Anything bad can be changed with the help of the Lord. There may be failures because we are all human beings and sinners; however, we can learn from our mistakes and become more united than ever if we make room for the Lord in our hearts. We are no longer under the power of sins and evil. In other words, this attempt at growth symbolizes the goodness of the Lord toward us. We should sing this goodness all the days of our lives. And it is a blessing to keep the joy of the faith in our heart. It also means that we know the way now. If we don't want to change, we will stagnate forever, we will fall and remain forever in our mediocrity. It is amazing to see how many people sometimes prefer to choose the path of pride and run away instead of making the effort to reestablish communication and build unity for the glory of the Lord. We all are human beings, not everything we think about or try to do will be right. However, if we do our best to always do things for the glory of the Lord, we will never falter. It is important to know that the glory of the Lord is different than the one chosen by men. Being the owner of the whole world, He decided to be born in a manger to teach us many lessons about our pride and the desire for applause. The humility shown to us by the example of Jesus is something that we should put into practice in everything we do. Only through humility in our way of living would we be able to sing praise to the Lord. The humble heart will always understand that he is called to grow day by day by listening to the words of God. When he fails, he will go with his head down in front of the Lord to ask him for forgiveness. The Scriptures and the faith say that whoever asks God for forgiveness will receive it. The Lord God does not hold grudges toward people. We, the human beings in this world, hold grudges sometimes out of pride because we think that we cannot fail. Pride is a bad habit which a believer should avoid to have. Lucifer was expelled from Heaven because of his pride. The reality is that there is no room in the kingdom of God for those who are proud, who hold grudges and who don't want to forgive others.

The Baptism Of The Lord Calls Us To Serve The Cause Of Peace

THE BAPTISM OF THE LORD in the Jordan opens a new chapter in the life of Jesus and brings a strong message of hope to humankind. It not only allows us all to become the brothers of Jesus when we receive the same Holy Spirit at our baptism, it also allows us to be His own in the world. We are marked with a seal which gives us a particular touch in our being. This allows us to be recognized as Children of God. This touch is made of love and forgiveness. As sinners we all can fail at a certain moment of our lives. We are not perfect and because of the weakness we carry within us, there is the possibility to cause disappointments in others. There will be disagreements between us, and whenever these moments occur in our lives, as Catholics, it is important for us to sit down and talk with the aim of resolving issues that may hurt us. That is one of the reasons why we go to Church and pray. We listen to God and learn from him so that we don't fall into temptation. The temptation is anything contrary to the Love, peace and unity that the Lord has brought to the world. The Lord does not want division among his children. Whenever there is a misunderstanding, He urges us to forgive those who have offended us and move forward. As Catholics and believers, this is the way to go and contribute to peace in the world. Wherever we can do that, we are laying a stone that will eventually help build peace in the world. The world does not know how to communicate and how to forgive. It encourages people to hold grudges and hunt for vindication until it reaches its goal: division. One of the challenges of the Catholic faith is that many faithful prefer to listen to the world and walk with it instead of choosing the path of reconciliation. Because of that limitation, the Lord does not want us to live our faith with the instructions coming from the world. On the day of His baptism, as it is for every one of us who wants to follow him, Jesus receives the Holy Spirit which allows Him to fulfill His mission. It is a grace that every man needs to receive in order for Him to be officially considered as a child of God and also as a follower of the Lord Jesus. The Holy Spirit gives Him the strength to face the challenges and the trials that He will encounter during the entire time He will spend doing the will of the Father. The will of the Father is that He spreads the good news to the whole world so that those who are part of it may learn how to love and how to carry their crosses. We all know how difficult it is to love, to welcome others, particularly those who are different. We all know how hard it is to put into practice the word of God. However, the Lord gives us all a second chance. If you really believe in love and peace, give a second chance to everyone who has offended you and this gesture will slowly bring peace into your heart.

Do Whatever He Asks You

THE CATHOLIC CHURCH IS A special organization which, contrary to many other religions, was founded by the Lord Jesus. Because of this particular touch we have in the faith, we have certainly some beliefs and some values that make us different in terms of our relationship with the Lord and our presence in the world. We are bound as Catholics to worship the Lord according to the teachings of the Ecclesial authorities from the Apostles to the fathers of the Church and from the different Councils to the Magisterium. Again, as we are exposed to so many interpretations coming from the world, it may be easy for us to be confused about the identity and the definition of a Catholic. The difficulty is that when Catholics are trapped in a world tainted with egocentricity and relativism, they tend to ignore the faith and what it is about. They think that they can be Catholics while they reject the beliefs and the values of the faith such as they are defined in the Gospel and in the Early Church. However, the messenger of the Lord who is represented in the person of the pope, the bishop and the priest, must teach the faith without modifying it. Therefore, the way to be Catholic is not by being a Cafeteria Catholic. It means that the habit in this modern age to fight with the messenger because he is preaching what he is supposed to say for the spiritual growth of the faithful is not the way to be Catholic. This is the attitude of the anti-Christ who is trying to impede the work of the Holy Spirit. A Catholic should never choose to be a minion of anti-Christ because there are grave consequences for the one who acts against the faith. God is the one who orders his messenger to spread the message. In that aspect, we all need to make efforts to spread the faith wherever we are. The Lord God will question those who are obstructing the truth in the instructions of faith. These instructions are explained in detail in the book of Catechism and touch upon many issues regarding our lives, taken from the Gospel, the Traditions and the counsels of early Christians. We all must know them and we are all encouraged to continue our religious education in learning many things from the faith in order to worship the Lord with one voice. It is a privilege to be a Catholic because we are the only divine institution that actually comes from the apostolic lineage. Therefore, when the Lord knocks at the door of our heart through the words of one of his messengers, we should not use violence towards him. We should open our heart and do our best to follow Him despite our weaknesses. The message is not there to cause us any harm. It is there to free us. Indeed, it may shake things up, however it is necessary because the Lord knows what is best for us. Do whatever He asks you.

THE PRESENCE OF GOD IN OUR LIVES BRINGS COMFORT TO US

THE INTIMATE PRESENCE OF GOD in every moment of our days gives us strength to accept our human condition as men and women, not perfect but as people of hope. We are called to do our best to walk behind the Lord in the journey He organized for us in this world and it is a long road. Some days may appear to be rougher than others, and we may feel that we are alone. However, the Lord is present, walking with us to give us support and stability. It is a pilgrimage that must be consecrated to the Lord and He is the only guide we can choose to lead us. In this journey, it is important that we nourish ourselves only with His word and His bread which will sustain us and give us the desire to pray for the others who also take part in the trip. Everyone is part of this quest. Some people may decide to get inebriated with the craziness of the world so that they may not experience the length of the trip and the various challenges that are part of it. Others may prefer to challenge it. The sad part of it is that they make it harder for themselves by choosing to protest against it. This is a part of one's human condition and it is not going to be easy. Nevertheless, it is a road filled with many surprises: ups and downs, and the Lord is the only one who knows what is ahead waiting for us before we reach our final destination. Though the mountains, the hills, the bad weather condition on the road may frighten us and we may be tempted to choose an easier path, it is important to follow the directions given by the Lord who wants to lead us. It is not an easy thing to do. We all have temptations and one way or another, there is the possibility for us to fail. However, we must come to our senses and return to the way that the Lord has set for us. Once you remain faithful to His command, you will understand that obedience to the Lord and to the faith are more important than anything else. On the last day of our life on earth, those two realities will be the only treasures we will carry with us. It is important to approach the faith with a spirit of obedience and fidelity so that we will join a community for the truth of the gospel and for the universality of the Church that is presented in this particular community. It is tragic to see today that the emphasis to join a parish will be put on a secular agenda where the priest tells jokes and where the people give praise, kisses and hugs, while disregarding the words of God and His Church. The problem is that if we are not challenged by the truth of the Scriptures, we will remain always in lies. In addition, whenever the cross comes to us, instead of sitting down to think and following the path of reconciliation we will be the first ones to hold grudges and to run away thinking that, where we are going, everything will be rosy and beautiful. The devil knows how to portray and paint things that way, giving us the lies that we want to hear so that we may feel good about ourselves and remain in our sins. He did the same thing to Adam and Eve. The purpose of coming to Mass is to worship the Lord and also to learn how to become a mirror of Christ here on earth. The question is how can we become Christ-like here on earth if we are not even ready to stop the gossip, the criticism, the disapproval, the jealousy, the unwillingness to forgive and to move forward?

Our Behavior As Adults Will Impact On The Future Of Our Children

W HEN THE LORD SPEAKS TO us, even with words that challenge our behavior and our lifestyle, His purpose is destined to gladden the heart and to invite us to a better life. The Lord will give His prophet the mission to deliver a message that invites the listener to change his heart and to repent of his evil doing. The listener is free to accept or to reject the Word, however the Lord reminds us that if you hear His voice today, harden not your heart. It means that the Lord expects something positive from the one to whom the message is proclaimed. Indeed, the purpose of God's word is to give us a second chance to amend our heart with the aim of saving our life. The Lord uses the prophet's mouth either to speak out by bringing comfort to those who are suffering or to denounce the sins that cause us to be far away from His commandments. That is where things become difficult and we all know that as human beings we don't like to be told what to do even though what is being said to us is the truth. We all know what happened to John the Baptist, after he told King Herod that he should not live in adultery. The Lord God does not want His prophets to be cowards who are afraid to speak His words and who are concerned about whether or not people love them. The Lord God wants them to spread the message that He orders them to do. This is a very difficult task particularly in a society where spirituality has been taken away from many sacred places and replaced with secular agenda. For example, every Catholic knows that you don't talk in church before or after Mass because of the presence of the Blessed Sacrament in the Tabernacle and because of charity and consideration we need to show toward those who are praying. For the one who knows the Catholic faith and wants to give priority to God, it is not an offense to request in a parish such a sacrifice for the Lord. With all that is happening in the world it is more than urgent for us to take the time to meditate in front of the Blessed Sacrament in order to converse with the Lord. When we do so, we find strength in our struggles; we will discover the beauty of the Catholic Faith, the importance to forgive and to move forward. We have seen that, in a world where there is no adoration and respect to the Blessed Sacrament where the house of the Lord is being transformed into a social market, and where people prefer noise than silence, there is a tendency for people to be artificial and superficial. Our Catholic traditions and our spirituality teach us how to maintain silence while we are in the house of the Lord. That is not an invention of the Church. Jesus always looked for a deserted place where He could pray silently. This has been our tradition because we have to give priority to God. The problem is that the enemy which is the anti-Christ will distract anyone from worshiping God and loving Him above all. However, there is no other way to be Catholic. There is one Faith, one Baptism, and one Lord who is God of all. If we take time to think about the role model we have to be for our children, we will understand that it is our responsibility to pass on the faith so that when we leave this world, we will be at peace with ourselves knowing that we have done our best to teach our kids and our grandkids the values and the beauty of the Catholic faith. If we teach them how to fight with priests because they are spreading the truth of the Gospel and the values of the Catholic faith, we have to question our own faith and ask ourselves and examine our conscience as to how we prepare our own children. However, if we teach them how to do their best to welcome the word of God even though they challenge them, if we teach them how to communicate with people particularly when there is conflict, how to sit down and with the help of the Lord, find a solution to preserve peace and unity. This way, we can be at peace with ourselves because we have given them the tools they need to save many relationships. In the end, it is important to know that the food we feed our children is the same they will use when they become adults. Therefore, we have to be careful about what we do in front of our children and grandchildren and how we model, so that they can emulate our good practices.

BEING ANOTHER CHRIST'S PRESENCE IN A COMMUNITY

WITH SO MUCH DIVISION GOING on in our world, we are supposed to be, as Catholics, another Christ's presence wherever we go. However it is not enough to have the slogan written in a mission statement; we must also put it into practice. That is the only way we will be credible and successful wherever we are. If we only use the words and are not opened to act like Jesus, it is all hypocrisy. It means a Catholic must be open to welcome the messenger of the Lord and the words he proclaims as a sign of blessing for his spiritual growth and not as a source of anger and suspicion to promote division. The devil always wants us to limit our faith to the little world we know as if everything about the faith or the Catholic Church should be decided inside this private and social group we have created. However, our Catholic Church is far beyond the customs of a parish, a group or a diocese. It is the holy, Catholic and apostolic Church which symbolizes the universality of the faith and the unity that exists among all who are a part of it. When we become members of the Catholic Church, we have to understand that we are not following a man but rather a Savior who gave His life on the cross for our salvation. When we follow the Lord with sincerity, whoever comes and speaks in the name of the Lord will always be welcome because he comes to help us enrich our faith and to help us remain faithful to the Lord. When we are influenced by the spirit of division, we expect that every messenger should act like a copy machine ignoring that every disciple chosen by the Lord brings a gift to a particular community, and if that leader dares act differently, he is quickly condemned and rejected. This is not an attitude encouraged by the Lord who made it very clear when sending His disciples into mission: Those who welcome you, welcome me and those who reject you reject me. The problem is when we are trapped in our little box we don't think outside of it and we forget about the spiritual responsibility that we all have. We must pray daily in order to grow in our faith. We must take the time to meditate when we come to Mass. The liberal agenda that some people want to promote inside the Catholic Church in this era is open to socialization and to talk inside the house of the Lord. They react negatively toward anything that is adoration and bristle at requests for complete silence in order to give priority to God and to hear the message He wants to provide everyone. When you see people who get offended because of a request to make the house of the Lord a house of prayer by taking some minutes to pray in silence in front of the Blessed Sacrament, it means that the enemy is present. Prayer is essential for the growth of not only our person but also for the welfare of the family. It is important for a family to sit at the table and pray together before meals and before going to bed. Those are the values that will maintain unity and consideration of each other as a brother or a sister. When the family is strong and willing to walk behind Jesus according to the values and the principles of the Catholic faith, then the community is blessed by numerous people who are not strangers to their faith. They will all understand the importance of prayer in a church particularly when the Blessed Sacrament is present. They will all support the priest building the house of the Lord into a house of prayer. It is easy to notice that the social market agenda and the liberal ideology that have been pushed by some individuals in some churches are not something good for the future of the Church. The problem with that kind of agenda is that it lacks compassion and charity. It may lead people to behaviors that are superficial and hypocritical where it is always somebody else's fault. It may encourage people to leave and go elsewhere especially when they don't get what they want instead of sitting down and preserving the bond of unity that is supposed to be there. However, the humble ones who put their trust in the Lord and who put themselves on their knees begging the Lord to come into their hearts are the ones who remain faithful both in good times and in bad times. They don't hold grudges; they hold a quietude which supports reverence. Indeed, that is the way we should live our faith, doing our best to follow the Lord by being humble and open to receive the food He brings to feed us.

THE SPECIFICITY OF THE
CATHOLIC FAITH

As CATHOLIC PEOPLE, WE ARE different and we must recognize that we have some particular beliefs which make us Catholic. Those values and beliefs have been handed down many centuries ago by the apostles to the early Christians who have given their lives to protect the faith. We cannot allow confused people to destroy these sacred traditions that have allowed us to be alive today. Our responsibility is to defend the faith and to pass those principles on to generations to come until the return of the Lord. It is not an easy task. Temptation is everywhere. As Catholics, we all need to improve our relationship with the Lord and with one another. We all need to increase our knowledge of the faith in order to worship the Lord in a better way and to better understand our responsibility as members of the Catholic Church. We should never take what we have for granted, all can disappear in a second. Because of that, we must rely only on the Lord and not on ourselves if we wish to continue to enjoy everything we have and all that we are. There is no point to waste our energy remaining in doubt and maintaining ideologies that cannot save us. There is a time when we must put away all that futility and surrender our total being to the Lord. Again, if we remain in that trap, we will never experience any other reality. The sad part of it is that we tend to believe that we are right. Indeed, that is a normal attitude if you never get out of your isolation. You can't give to people what you don't have. Once we experience the love of God in our lives, we will discover that we must be good to others and we cannot continue to be bitter or mad at people indefinitely because life is too short. We must trust God and always put everything into His hands. In each culture, there are things that contribute to the development of the person. At the same time, there are customs that are not fruitful or simply contribute to mediocrity. That is the reason why, today, the future of the world is not in closing ourselves in a little shell where everyone does the same thing in term of values, drink the same thing or eat the same thing. The future of our world is in the changing of heart, no matter who we are. It is the time to be open in the Lord and to others, and we all can learn from one another. No matter how old we are, there must be room for improvement, for continued education and open mindedness so that we may always remain open to perceive the marvels of the Lord who can amaze us. The worst thing is to believe that our own custom and beliefs are the best and that there is no other alternative. The things of the faith are not culturally bound; we can confidently believe that there is One God, one faith, one Church and one Catechism. Everything else depends on the culture, the education and the environment in which we grew up. However, our Catholic faith, by its very nature, is the guardian of principles that will ensure the dignity of every person and help anyone to change his heart and thus contribute to a world where there is less greed, violence and wickedness. Through faith every person who lives on this planet should have the desire and the will to change his heart. We were all, according to the reality, created by the same God who has blessed us with the gift of conscience where He communicates with us and because we all have the same destiny: death. We are all brothers and sisters and, therefore, there is no need to remain in those ideologies we carry in our heads. Through faith, the world would be a better place for all. The thing that impedes peace and justice in the world is that people don't want to change their hearts and we have fabricated our own misery.

THE NECESSITY OF PRAYER

MORE THAN EVER, IN THIS era where there are some people with personal agendas who want to establish a Church where anything goes, we need to pray because it is an attack from the enemy who is trying to confuse people and create division. Prayer is the key to respond positively to God's call and also to face those threats toward the faith, the institution of the Church and particularly the family. Family is the basis for the future of a better world where children can learn about stability, love and forgiveness. When they become adults, they will certainly contribute to a world where there is less greed and less violence. It is important for us to do what it takes to protect the family and the values that go with it. In a time where some people even refuse to be called sinners because of their determination to defy the teachings of the Church, we have the urgency to turn to the Lord and ask for His help. Prayer will allow us to give testimony to the faith and to become people who are sincere and profound with manners and principles that are rooted in the Lord and in the Catholic Traditions. It will give people more awareness of the presence of God not only among those who think the same way but in every person. In the end, we will discover that God has created one man and one woman. The only difference is that custom and culture play a big role in shaping behaviors and styles. It is important to develop the habit of prayer in our life in order to understand the truth of our life and to become people of hope blessed with the gift of patience. And, it is visible, because of lack of true prayer that people tend to hold grudges and destroy bonds that existed between them. People who don't pray don't know how to welcome others who are not part of their circle and they fail to promote good communication. But such a lifestyle has failed to contribute to the expansion and the unity of the Church. In other words, it has failed to evidence the Catholicity of the Church. It is easier to find more openness and more compassion for others among the Catholics who are obedient to the faith and who include prayer in their lives. In addition, it seems evident that more vocations to the priesthood and to the religious life are present in those communities where people are clearly faithful to the teachings of the Church and the apostolic Traditions and where they pray more. The problem with those who claim to have an agenda of disobedience to the Church is that once you don't share their ideologies, it seems they lack charity and quickly exclude those who don't share their attitudes from everything and fail to show mercy. It is high time to make an evaluation and realize that the future of the Church is more on the side of those who are humble and open to remain faithful to the Teachings of the faith because at least its members are open to promote vocations to the priesthood and value the complementary role of the clergy and laity. The pride and disobedience agenda has not brought anything deep and good for the faith. On the contrary, we have seen a bunch of unhappy people who are difficult and, in their ministries, they sow confusion and doubt in the truth and love that Christ wants all to know and share. When the reverence is gone, anything goes. In all of this, the Church is moving forward with the aim of bringing us closer to God. In the end, the Lord will prevail.

The Face Of The Lord Is Pure; In Him, There Is No Hypocrisy

As Christians, it is always a duty for us to be grateful to the Lord God for everything He has done for us. We must consistently recognize the goodness of the Lord in our lives and that is a beauty we need to nurture and spread around particularly in this season of grace given to us to reform our lives. This is not the time to be sad as if we were miserable people; this is the time of salvation where we are called to find out more about our identity. We are dust and to dust we will return says the scripture. It is not any kind of dust. It is a dust that has been renewed by the Lord God, through the faith, through His Church and through the sacraments. We have been fashioned by the love of God and with the dust mixed with the water poured upon us at our Baptism, we become a new creature that will contribute to build the Kingdom of love and unity among us in this world and in the world to come. We must recognize that we have been blessed and the fact that we are alive and being exposed to all of these spiritual blessings allowing us to be better people, not asking for more is testament of such blessing. Anyone who accepts to be challenged by the words of God will have the reward of eternal life. When we accept to be criticized by the words of God, we become aware of our weaknesses and our shortcomings and gradually the Holy Spirit comes to us and helps us detach ourselves from those things that disguise our true identity. We have been created in the image of God and we all have the capability to love and to forgive. If we cannot, either love or forgive another person, it means that we have been influenced by the devil and the love of God is not in us. God is love and because of this love, He forgave those who did crucify him and He died on the Cross to show us the way. Therefore, when people come to Mass and are disturbed because the words of God challenge them in their lifestyle made of impatience, gossiping, hypocrisy and violence, they become mad. It means they are not really in tune with their own identity. It is important to socialize, it is wonderful to laugh. However, the faith reminds us that we come to the house of the Lord to praise and worship Him, not to entertain ourselves. We come to praise Him who is the Lord of Heaven and Earth. We come to the source of love to fill our tank so that we may know how to live our relationships with one another. We come to receive strength so that we may face the trials and difficulties that surround us, to ask forgiveness for our sins, for our moments of doubt and for our weaknesses at all levels. We also come to thank Him for everything He has given us and to receive strength from Him in order to continue our journey. The new religion which is trying to switch the purpose of the celebration by giving way to our personal tastes instead of God, is not encouraged by the Catholic Faith. It is something coming from the enemy. When the devil sees that you are trying to please God, to be faithful to Him, he knows how to discourage you by saying to you that you will fail because you are worthless. At the same time, when he sees that you are not really interested in spirituality and that you are more inclined to society, he knows how to get you and make you believe that everything you do is OK and you should indulge yourself more than praise God. Such a behavior causes people to be difficult. Nevertheless, everything has been given to us: human life, forgiveness for our sins, eternal life. However, we have insatiable hunger for other things. The Lord God offers us a life of holiness made of peace, unity and love. But, we chose to look for division, violence and hypocrisy. It is amazing to see how many people fall into this trap. The enemy is very good about inculcating into our minds that there is final bliss. This season also allows us to catch up a little bit. It concerns all of us who have been behind in our relationship with the Lord. Another chance is given to us so that we may reform our lives. Should we ignore this opportunity and remain in our pride and our ideologies? No, let us grab this excellent opportunity to focus only on God.

It Is Healthy For Us To Change Our Hearts

As human beings, we all, at a moment of our life, have had an urgency or a situation where we needed the support of someone but there was no one who could really help us. Those moments whenever they occur, if we are not strong, can bring frustration and loneliness or, worse, despair, since we may feel totally isolated. This is where you are called to call upon the Lord and look for His help; He is there waiting for you, because you are His child. Being the Father, someone who is compassionate and caring, He is the only one who can respond totally to you and without any reservations. Indeed, He is the only one who will be there for you, to help you go to the other side. No matter how close you can be to a person, no matter how much love a person can have for you, God is the only one who has the means to give you peace on the last day. That is the reason why you have no other choice than to surrender yourself totally to Him and ask for His mercy. As believers, we have been taught to turn to God in our moments of sorrows and tribulation. We have been asked to do our best not to judge so that we don't get judged on the day of the return of the Lord. We have been encouraged to promote unity and to forgive those who have offended us. Those are the multiple tasks that, among others, we need to do while we are still blessed by the Lord to be alive. To believe in God and to surrender to Him is an act of humility. It is a process and we must start now. In fact, where else can we go? God is the first person to whom we have to direct our call particularly when we have to face the reality of illness. There are some diseases that are transitory: there are others that are terminal. Every one of us will experience this truth sooner or later. Once you are born, you will have to go through it and there is nothing you can do to avoid it. This can be a very scary experience if you don't have a relationship with the Lord. Whenever we are in perfect health, we assume that we are invulnerable and we are in this world until a ripe old age. The same thing occurs when we have power, whether it be power from being a leader of a nation or power because we are not sick. God always answers our calls in many ways. We may receive help from a friend, a spouse or a member of the family, an institution etc.[...], however, it is God in action through those people. But the faith we have allows us to believe that He is also present in the Church which is His House. Indeed, the Lord being the creator of Heaven and Earth is everywhere but, most particularly, He is in the celebration of the Eucharist, He is in our hearts, He is in the Sacraments and, finally, He is in the Tabernacle. When we come to Church, this is where we go to converse with the Lord, heart to heart to tell Him everything. The human heart has been created by God and that is the reason why the heart cannot hide anything from God. When we talk to God with a sincere heart and tell Him everything, He will give us a blessing which calls for a changing of heart. If we do what He asks us to do, then we enter in a relationship with Him. At that moment, there is a transformation made within us that can be noticed by others. We become more relaxed and more patient and anger will dissipate, as demonstrated in our attitudes and outlook in life. The transformation realized within us is capable of reaching others and, suddenly, we become messengers and prophets who contribute to the spreading of the goodness of the Lord in our world. We must trust God's will with all our hearts and all our minds whole heartedly.

A PERFECT TIME FOR
RECONCILIATION

WHO IN THIS LIFE HAS not been hurt or offended by someone? Oftentimes, the utterance of words is not necessary so as to offend someone. The fact you don't share someone's ideologies and beliefs can be a source of distraction and anger. This world is a very complicated place to live in, particularly when you are dealing with people who decide to have beliefs that are not in harmony with the words of God. We have been witnesses, in recent years how fanatism on the part of the faithful can push people to adopt behaviors that are destructive not only for others but also for themselves. One bad thing about fanatism is that whoever decides to follow its agenda suddenly becomes irrational and it is impossible for that person to have a dialogue with anyone. The person who is fanatical does not use logic but rather emotions to communicate and to make his point. Most of the time, the fanatic defends an ideology because he believes this cause to be true according to the taboos of the education he received. However, the Lord brings us a passion for the truth which is not an ideology. It is the bread of life that everyone needs to survive. Because of this nourishment for our own spiritual and personal growth, we have a basis on which we can rely upon in order to be strong people who will be witness to the truth, people who are open to make sacrifices and who are not afraid to carry the cross for the Lord. To do everything for the Glory of the Lord is the key for a good outlook toward life in general, toward charity and even forgiveness. When you have had a bad experience at a moment of your life and it is nagging in your head, pushing you to be angry or to hate the person who has initiated it, it is time for you to talk to the Lord and ask for His help. When we decide to maintain hatred in our hearts and are not willing to love and forgive, we are harming ourselves. Whoever decides to hold grudges against another person has chosen to be miserable, because when we don't forgive others, we are damaging ourselves by letting this poison cause us to be disturbed and to be negative. Only people who love themselves can forgive others, because in putting into practice something that is good, we choose to reward ourselves. Forgiveness brings liberation to the soul and to the mind. Choosing not to forgive is a heavy burden you should not let weigh in your heart. It does not merit anyone. It is truly extra baggage for the devil who is delighted to have someone on his side and who is likewise trapped and unable to free himself thus making it impossible to enjoy the invitation of the Lord to love and to forgive, for God is love. Despite the fact that many people say their morning and evening prayers every day, they recite the Our Father and they even say the part where Jesus reminds us: "and forgive us our trespasses as we forgive those who trespass against us" but they ignore the implication of such a powerful message in the prayer. However, in Mt. 6: 7-15, the Lord makes it very clear: [....]. Yes, if you forgive others their failings, your Heavenly Father will forgive you yours; but if you do not forgive others, your Father will not forgive your failings either". The question is this: Which part of the prayer can we identify ourselves with? What do we gain by promoting division among us? It is the time to realize that there is no better place than the one the Lord has designed for you to be in. The point is that wherever you go, the Cross will follow you. You may not see it at the beginning, but you must be prepared for it because, it will come; there is no real life without the Cross. Some people choose to ignore it, and create an environment of lies where everything is set to make them feel good. It is just a façade. It is all a hoax. It is time to be real about our faith, to feed ourselves with real food from the Scriptures, God's words which challenge us. It is time to come back to the Lord, to come back to the place where we belong. Let us not just babble. Let us mean it when we tell people that we love them. Indeed, there is no love without the Cross. This is the time to stay away from those lies that are there only to make us feel good and complacent while we stay away from the doctrinal basis that we all need to be another real "Christ" here in our world as Jesus is real and alive. Let us nurture these good practices.

Love Is The Newness That
The Lord Expects From Us

LOVE IS THE KEY FOR a good relationship with the Lord as well as with others; however, it is not just any kind of love. It is the love that will allow a person to be faithful despite the difficulties and trials he may encounter in his life. It is the love that will not dissipate when challenged to change our lives and to make progress into the path of holiness. It is an authentic love that will allow a person to lay down his life for his friends. Jesus came and accepted to die on the cross to show us how much he loves us so that we may learn how to love. We all need to enter into this deep love in order for us to experience the meaning of our existence. It is important for us to know how to love not just verbally but to love sincerely so that it may last forever. Many believers, because of the love they have found in the Lord, have given their treasures and used their wealth to help others, to embellish the creation of God, to follow Jesus' footsteps. Some fulfill these duties by going to the missions around the world. Those who cannot go, decide to be another Christ wherever they are and whoever they become. They are not bitter people nor frustrated or controlling. They give their time, their presence to contribute to a better place in their environment. Surprisingly, they remain quiet and very discreet. They welcome whoever comes along in their way and they really wish for the success of others. This kind of love they have for the people of God is a blessing for those who live around them. However, we have also been challenged by situations that remind us about the carrying of a cross and the Lord makes it very clear: unless you carry your cross behind me you cannot be my disciple.

That is the reason why we should never be discouraged, particularly in the presence of the cross. We are called to be faithful to our commitments in whatever area of our lives. It is not wise to say to someone that we love him/her only when things are going well; it is essential to understand that true love requires the presence of the cross where our love will be tested. If the love we have for a person or our community is purely emotional, it will be fleeting, and whenever there is a difficulty, we will run away, destroying the bond that supposedly was there. We will be the first one to blame the other and not willing to accept our contribution to the situation. Indeed, fidelity is a virtue that we need in our lives. Our God is a faithful God who will never change His love for us no matter what we do. If we repent and ask Him for forgiveness, He will forgive us and He will not turn His back away from us. Where else are you going to find such a deal? Today, our world needs to focus more on these principles and values that have been forgotten, we need to restore our love for God and others. We have adopted other manners that are not helpful to build the kingdom of God which is love, forgiveness and humility. Instead, we have seen a desire for vengeance and wickedness, criticism and ill will. We have seen behaviors that promote holding grudges rather than forgiving others. Nevertheless, we have to put such a confusion into the hands of God, because it is sad for a person to reach that level of life where he tends to reinforce behaviors that are unforgiving. If we are the followers of the Lord, we cannot continue to be people who are unforgiving and quick to condemn. It is so easy to be judgmental while we miss the point. It is important to be reminded that being judgmental is a sign of immaturity. There are so many of us who fall in this kind of distraction and we think that we are right. The Lord Jesus comes to show us a new way that invites us to be patient and slow to judge. No matter how old we are, there must be room for improvement otherwise we will be adults but we will not grow spiritually. Indeed, it takes a lot of humility for a person to recognize his failure and to accept guidance. Only a person who listens to God can accept to be challenged by His words with the purpose of being a better person. Only the love for Jesus can allow a person to forgive others. Only the love for the Lord can help us. Try it and all will change for you.

THE POSITIVE ASPECT
OF SUFFERING

I N THIS WORLD OF TODAY, suffering is being perceived as a punishment for something that we have done. For reasons unknown, it is connected to something that is negative and hurtful. Thus, man should not suffer. Particularly, when we see children who are suffering, or the elderly who spend many years struggling with some kind of diseases in the hospitals or nursing homes, we are touched by their pain, and death seems much more acceptable than to go through such sufferings. Perceived in a pagan context, suffering is really inhuman. People should not suffer and we want them all to be happy without any cross to carry. The problem with this kind of belief is that it is dangerous for our faith and also with such an interpretation, it will be impossible for anyone to maintain fidelity to the Lord and to those who live around us. Since suffering is being interpreted as a curse upon us, people try to escape from it as much as they can in order to receive happiness, to free themselves from something that is not helping them to fulfill their dream. Because of our inability to see the positive side of suffering, many relationships at family, friendship and community level have been attacked, destroyed and broken. People have made many promises to one another but, because of a disagreement or the emergence of problems between them, everything has turned into a type of suffering. It raises question of integrity when a person decides to desist and to believe that brushing the problems aside will allow him to experience a life without sufferings. Such an attitude toward suffering is not the way for us to face the reality of God's will. If we approach suffering with a negative point of view where we don't want to be part of it, it will bring a lot of pain and a lot of unpleasant surprises when and if we reach old age. As we get older, the body does not function in the same way as it did when we were in our twenties. The reality of arthritis and many other things will invade our body and sometimes there is no medicine that can really help us to be pain free. It means the time will come when whether we like it or not, we will face the reality of life's passages and we will have to rely only on God in order to find our hope and strength to move forward. Suffering should be taken as a part of our life and not as a curse. In a Christian context, we should do our best to help those who are suffering particularly the poor, the sick and the orphan. We must be compassionate to anyone who is in need. With all of this, suffering can bring empathy towards people contributing to love and peace. When we never suffer in our lives, it may be easy for us to become spoiled and not tolerant enough to endure adversities. We may take everything for granted and even destroy our own happiness. How many young men and women who could have been very successful have jeopardized their future because they did not listen to their parents, grand parents or their friends? Instead of listening to them, they run away from the house and get involved in bad things because they did not want to endure the little crosses at home. So, to endure sufferings in your life, particularly the ones you encounter while growing up, can bring a lot of wisdom and maturity for the future. Jesus who is God, went through the ultimate suffering with humility of heart and acceptance. He did nothing wrong. This question that we constantly raise toward God: "Why me"? can be felt and answered through the Passion of the Lord, His Crucifixion and His Resurrection. He accepted to suffer so that we may learn how to face the reality of suffering which is not a punishment but rather an opportunity for virtue, a time to call upon the Father and to rely on Him. Many of us will change our hearts only when we will be hit by something hard; otherwise, we prefer to remain in our own utopias which cannot really save us. But for the one who wants to trust, to obey and to be faithful, he does not need to wait for a big catastrophe for him to be humble, to change his heart and to follow the Lord. Every day of his life will be considered as a blessing where the Lord, through the Church, is the only teacher who can really fortify his soul and instruct him as to how to conduct his life. In order to reach this

Fr. Joseph Bellerive, JCD

level of faith, we need first to be humble and not be so obstinate and self important that we develop a kind of attitude where we don't want to be told the truth of the Gospel. Life is short. We should not waste it arguing over things that are interpretations of some people who have lost the true faith which is a gift from God. The guidance of the Church is there for our own peace of heart and our salvation. Let us embrace it with humility, doing our best to live it and give the rest to the Lord. It is a better deal for us to accept it than to protest against it.

GET OUT OF YOUR TOMB

THE RESURRECTION OF JESUS IS one of the most significant demonstrations of God's love in our lives. It is something so special that there is no word to describe it. Jesus, after enduring all the difficulties of the Cross, after being faithful and obedient to His Father, was rewarded the gift of the Resurrection. It is something that concerns not only Jesus but everyone who accepts to follow Him. It is the ultimate grace that is attributed to the Son of God because of his humbleness and the willingness to do His Father's will. Everyone who follows the steps of Jesus carrying his cross without frustration but with confidence will see the marvels of the Lord in the land of the living. The Resurrection of the Lord is a call to all of us who have abandoned the true faith, all of us who are tempted to follow other leaders who cannot save us so that we may reflect upon the importance of doing the Father's will. As we get older, it is important for us to surrender ourselves to the Lord and increase our faith in order to experience the peace that He came to bring to us and that we can all attain. It is essential that we synchronize our age with the amount of faith we possess for a deeper relationship with the Lord through His Church. As we reach old age and we realize that we are not quite at ease with the teachings of the faith, we have the moral obligation to examine ourselves and our consciences to resolve the situation. We must grow not only physically in age, but we must also mature in wisdom and in the faith. The truth is that everything in this world is passing. We will leave all our possessions behind. Nothing is truly lasting. It is important for us as an authority figure in the family to set the good example and to be good models. As a parent or grandparent, this is the time to be a light for the family. Children and grandchildren look up to these models and the authority in the family. They need reference. This is not the time to rebel against the faith. On the contrary, we should take the opportunity to be grateful to the Lord for He has done everything for us. Now that we are blessed with so many things: money, health, accomplishment, this should be the moment to glorify the Lord by supporting the faith so that the younger generation can have a foundation on which to build their lives. The enemy will always try to tempt people to complain, protest or rebel against many issues that are part of our faith. However, it is beneficial for us to understand the tricks of the enemy. If a person thinks that the Church is not expressing the truth and that his/her own opinion is the truth, it becomes an enormous issue. Some individuals think that the Church, as an organization, built on the faith of St. Peter as a rock, followed and maintained by several ecclesial authorities, cultures and customs and beliefs through several gatherings (called councils) to reach a conclusion about the veracity of a dogma, can fail. How can a person, limited by his own little world, isolated in his own thinking, try to introduce his individual opinion upon the faithful as the truth? How much more can personal opinion be in error? It means that if we are obedient to the faith, we will have the light to identify the true and the false teaching and, whenever an isolated person who is not an authority of the Church gives an opinion about a practice in the faith, we have to use a lot of logic not to be confused with such interpretation with others. In addition, it is also our responsibility to defend the faith and even to guide those who tend to go astray, our lost sheep. There is one Lord, one Church, one Faith. To be a Catholic means to accept and live the teachings contained in the entire package coming from the Catholic Church. The enemy who has given his personal opinion to Adam and Eve and has brought confusion in the whole world continues to look for more disciples. If our faith is strong, our foundation concrete, we will not listen to the enemy but if we are weak, we will be tempted to believe the interpretation of the enemy whose purpose is to bring division. We wonder why there is so much division in the world and even in the Church. The Resurrection of Jesus invites us all to a new life: unity among us as brothers and sisters and also unity in the faith under one authority which is the Church. By doing so, we will have the will to continue to carry our crosses and through patience and endurance we too will be risen. Christ is risen, let us do our best not to remain in the nefariousness of divisions but rather feed ourselves with the faith in the risen Lord who came to unite us all together with His Body and Blood. Let us do our best to rise with Him by remaining faithful to Him and to learning from Him what obedience and fidelity mean in our lives, in our relationship with one another and particularly in our relationship with God. With this particular sign of love for us manifested in His Resurrection, we have definitely the reasons to get out of our tombs particularly the tombs of negativity and criticism in which we are buried. It is more important to focus on the sufferings of Jesus, and His resurrection after His death. This is the best way we will experience the strength needed to face the multiple difficulties of our daily life. It is our gift, our only gift.

The Resurrection Of The Lord: Symbol Of Mercy And Compassion

One of the most precious fruits of the Resurrection of the Lord as His gift to the world is peace. Jesus came to bring Peace to the whole of humanity, particularly to those who decide to follow Him. The future of humanity resides in peace, where in the name of the Lord, people from different nations, cultures and social backgrounds can live as brothers and sisters. Wherever there is a possibility, people should not be quick to condemn others because they are different. Peace will come from the openness for us to wait before making harsh judgments. Only those who live the faith properly and sincerely will welcome others in the name of the Lord. It means when we live the faith not with emotions, rather with convictions, we will be less quick to say things that we don't know. This way, we will reach peace with others. It is this peace that is announced by the prophet Isaiah through which the cow and the bear make friends, the calf and the lion cub feed together and they do not harm each other. It means that married couples who have different personalities, if the Peace of the Lord is present in their hearts, can experience togetherness and live in love and harmony. Indeed the same thing can occur between people from different customs and races, when the peace of the Lord remains in them; they live in harmony and respect one another without any reservations and undue sensitivities. Without this peace, there is no happiness for man because conflict and division don't benefit the human heart. On the contrary, they bring sadness and anxiety. Peace is our objective: we need to strive for it, work on it and nurture it as we continue our journey here on earth following the steps of the Lord crucified. Peace can only be attained through obedience to the will of the Father and through humility carrying the crosses of life behind Jesus. The contact with Jesus invites us to peace and it is more than the absence of conflicts. It is life itself manifested in the daily activities of our life. When people are blessed with the Peace of the Lord in their heart, they reflect it through their kindness, their generosity and their sincerity. It is a part of them to know how to communicate and how to be patient. However, when the Peace of the Lord is lacking in the heart of a person, it can be apparent through the way that person relates to others, accepts or rejects the challenges that come to him and manifested in one's whole make-up. A life without the Peace of the Lord cannot satisfy the human heart, but a life filled with peace is a gift from God. Whoever is a person of peace in a relationship, in a family or in a group is a blessing. It is a tribute to have him/her around. Who is the peace person in the family? There must be a person in the family who is the Peace person to calm things down especially when a member of the family tends to go off on a tangent. Peace is a virtue that we constantly need to nurture with the purpose of showing love and compassion to others. The event of the Resurrection shows us the Mercy and Compassion of the Lord in our lives. In a world where we justify everything we do, in a society where we always blame somebody else for our shortcomings, the resurrection of the Lord invites us to be people who show mercy to others. As human beings, there is going to be disagreement between us. But, we don't have to walk away from another because of a conflict. Through His Passion and Crucifixion, the Lord Jesus has shown us how to resolve those kinds of situations. Before He died on the Cross and to all those who betrayed, mistreated and crucified Him, He said to the Father: "Father, forgive them, they don't know what they do". This is what we are called to do as followers of the Lord whenever we find ourselves in a situation of conflicts, we are called to forgive if we want to experience peace. How do we welcome the peace of the Lord in our lives? How do we share this peace with other people? In order to be a person of peace to those who live around us, it is essential that we first have peace with ourselves. God is the only one who can give us that peace. So, if we are not at peace with God and with ourselves, we will never be at peace with others. Peace can come in our hearts only when we trust God more than anything else. Peace can also be present within us when we are charitable and sincere. If we are judgmental people, hypocritical and quick to be angry, we will never experience the peace the Lord is talking about. The Peace of the Lord is associated with His Mercy and Compassion for all of us.

BLESSED ARE THOSE WHO BELIEVE WITHOUT SEEING

THE RESURRECTION OF THE LORD invites us to something that appears to be impossible. Blessed are those who believe without seeing. How can a person trust someone that he has never seen physically? How can you believe something that is transmitted to you when the world is saying something different from what Jesus says? It takes not only trust and humility to have faith. It also takes an immense offering of our control to surrender our brain to God and allow the Church to shepherd our lives. For more than two thousands years, people from every nation, intelligent people who have accomplished a lot of marvels in the world and in the Church, have believed the truth of the Gospel and have followed the Lord. People from all kinds of social background have given their lives to the Lord by believing all the teachings He entrusted to the Church, they continue to fortify themselves with prayers, receiving the Holy Eucharist and devotions. Millions of young people have had several encounters with the Lord to the point that they have chosen to die rather than to reject their faith: Among them, Maria Goretti, Joan of Arc and many others. All of those philosophers such as Thomas of Aquinas, Edith Stein, Jacques Maritain and his wife Raïssa have contributed enormously to the faith. They could have decided not to believe because they were intelligent, famous and gifted. However, having found the answers to their many questions regarding the state of man after death, they have accepted to embrace the Catholic faith and they never questioned it. Most of them were not raised in the Catholic Faith but through their humility, they believed and became new and renewed individuals. So, it requires a lot of logic in order to shape our faith and make it a source of strength for ourselves. It also takes a lot of humility to be open enough and learn from the masters, the ones who have given their lives with joy and who are happy in serving the Lord and to know His will. If we are going to nurture our faith from the interpretation of those who are not at peace with themselves, they are not going to help us. If we are going to build our faith by listening to those people who are confused about their choices in life or are frustrated about many things that are happening in their lives and they are very critical about the institution and the organization of the Church, we will endanger our faith. We will become difficult people who will never be a channel of peace to others until we make that commitment to accept the faith and to put everything into the hands of the Lord, entirely in God's Holy Will. This is exactly what Jesus did. In the face of all the challenges of His life in which He was betrayed, mistreated and crucified, Jesus turned to His Father for strength and guidance. So, if we are experiencing doubt about some elements of our Catholic faith, it is wise to turn to God and receive instructions from Him so that we may receive in our hearts His holy instructions. This is the challenge to which the Resurrection of the Lord is calling us. It is inviting us to trust and obey the Father from whom we can receive the supreme reward for our effort. The event of the Resurrection is asking us to have a greater faith. Faith is a necessary element for a human being to have. Without faith, the Lord's resurrection is meaningless. Faith in God adds something to our life that no one on earth can provide to us. It is most fundamental to have a faith that is sincere, a faith that does not question for the sake of curiosity, a faith that seeks in order to know better. The Resurrection of the Lord is the fundamental element of our faith. There is no need for things to be tangible, because there is nothing that can stop God's life. There is only one word to believe, the one initiated and testified by the disciples. It brings joy and peace not only to the world but also to our hearts. It is a crucial element for the success of our relationship with one another. Without it, we will always be confused. We will always be disturbed and quick to reject the truth of the Scriptures. We only need to trust more in order to experience that joy and that peace brought by Jesus Christ risen from the dead. Let us deepen our faith, renew our faith without any interference from man who cannot give us salvation. Our lives would truly change if we work at it and give it all we have.

THE NEW LIFE BROUGHT BY JESUS RISEN FROM THE DEAD

NOW THAT JESUS IS RISEN from the dead, have we been risen with Him? Are we renewed with positive attitude to change our heart in cooperating with the Lord so that we may have a better life? Are we ready to glorify the Lord in everything we do? Are we committed to speak out for the Lord and believe in His word? Indeed, the Resurrection of the Lord invites us to a change of heart and a growth in our faith. If, in the past, we were unable to have hope and trust, now that we have seen the marvels of the Lord through His resurrection, we have to get rid of all negativity and be more positive about everything concerning our lives. We have to be people of dialogue, ready to communicate the word that builds and creates something new for the Glory of the Lord. In a world where there is a lot of resistance to conversion, the Resurrection of the Lord is calling us to change our lives, to rise and to direct our thoughts to things that are from above. May everything we say to one another bring consolation, comfort and peace so that we all can be another Jesus in our community, in our world. One of the impediments to sharing peace with others is selfishness because the emphasis in our world is more on the side of me....me. However, as Catholics, if we take our faith seriously and are open to the truth of the Gospel, there are many things we can do. The difficulty for our faith today is that some members of the Catholic Church instead of nurturing themselves with the words of God transmitted to the Church via the apostles and preserved through the testimonies of the early Christians, prefer to go astray regarding the faith. They have their own interpretation regarding the faith. The confusion is that they associate such a behavior as a sign of being smart, someone who understands the words of God better than the rest of the faithful. Let us avoid such competitions. Such an attitude in a pastoral setting cannot bring peace but division. There is one faith and, as Catholics, we all are bound by it. The enemy can do his work by creating in us a rebellious attitude toward the teachings of the Church as if we could save ourselves without the direction of the Church. This is a dangerous way to live our faith because the history of our salvation since Moses has been always presented under the guidance of a leader. All the prophets have received a mission to lead and guide the people of God. The disciples were sent into mission and they all had a specific responsibility. The Church is the new prophet. So, how can some members of this generation have the illusion that salvation can be done through their personal interpretation? It is not a personal interpretation but rather a task that needs to be accomplished: to spread the Good News of the Lord. If we think only about our wants and forget about obedience and humility to the words of God, we will never contribute to a world of peace. The Lord God is counting on every one of us to continue bringing love to the world by accepting to explore the richness of our affiliation to Jesus and His Church. It is difficult to get rid of the old being within us particularly if we are resisting the challenges that the faith is bringing to us. Each one of us is given a gift from God; we should use this particular gift to change our lives, our behavior and all our being. We should become a new creature in the Lord so that we may experience the peace that the Lord has brought through His resurrection. In doing so, people who are living with us will touch the goodness of the Lord in the way we treat them. Whatever part of our being needs a change, we should do it: we should rise above negativity in which we tether ourselves. When we start our Lenten season, most of us have promise Heaven and Earth to the Lord. We have said that we would do more effort to please Him, to spend more time with the family, to cut out our prejudices or to pray more fervently. However, as time goes by, we realize that it is not an easy thing to do because we repeat the same mistakes again. When the same bad habits occur, the temptation is to believe that we are good for nothing and there is no need even to go to confession because we confess the same sins over and over. Such a reaction toward our faults is not encouraged by the Church or by spirituality because it is the voice of the enemy trying to tell us not to trust in God and to remain prisoners of our weaknesses. The point is that, even though we have made promises to the Lord and that we have fallen, there is no need to panic because our Lord is a merciful Lord, slow to anger and full of compassion. If we are faithful to the faith, the Lord knows that our desire is to follow him; however, we need humility to go to Him; whenever, we fail. Where else can we go? One thing that we must know is that the change we want to be accomplished in our life will not come at the moment we are expecting but rather at the unexpected moment which is the moment of the Lord. Let us wait for that moment with patience and self control. Let us keep this thought and attitude in our hearts daily through prayers.

Jesus Is Our Good Shepherd

THE CHURCH IS THE HOUSE of God among men. It is the place of Catholic gatherings and the sign of God's presence in our lives. It is also the domain where we receive instructions for our spiritual journey here on earth so that we may have the strength to face all the challenges on the roads ahead. Indeed, without the Lord's help, there is no way we can keep on going. Even in the Church, we will find difficulties which sometimes put our faith to the test: the Church is the House of the Lord designed to bring us comfort and hope. We, who are its members, are called through our actions and attitudes to make its beauty radiant and welcoming for everyone. The Church is more than a social club where we choose and pick people we want to be with. Because of its divine nature, the Church is the place where we come to celebrate our faith in God through the help of the Holy Spirit. Once we understand the purpose of our presence in the Church, we would never be upset about the truth of the Gospel. God is the Alpha and the Omega, the beginning and the end. God is above all things and we are expected that we should love him that way. These symbols should also be expressed in our liturgy so that Honor and Glory be dedicated to the Lord and not to our egos. Respectful for those who are praying to God before and after Mass, we should not raise our voices inside the church. We are not in a social club. It is easy to lose the reverence and the spiritual atmosphere that we all are invited to create in the Church. We all know that reverence is something we must pay. The problem is that when we put the emphasis on the social aspect of the gathering, we forget that the Lord is in charge of the place. We spend more time talking to each other in a loud manner instead of talking to the Lord. In doing so, it is easy for us to become empty and superficial, away from the true faith. In that kind of setting, it will always be difficult for a person who acts that way to forgive and to be compassionate and to lose perspective. Through the sacraments we receive in the Church, we all are bound to contribute to the beauty of the House of the Lord and to invite all people to follow Him. It is a task which will bring us internal healing since everything in this world is temporary. Only the Lord will remain forever. In our own lives, it is so clear that everything we have will disappear. One by one, we all will leave this world and we will go alone. The last thought we will have in this world should be directed to God, because in that particular moment, we all will cry out to God asking Him to forgive us. So, when the Church encourages us to put God first in our lives, it is not trying to be dominant over us or trying to make our lives difficult. On the contrary, it is preparing us for the big day that all of us will face. There is nothing we will be able to do. Nobody, not even the person we love, the social group we were always part of, will be able to deliver us. God is the only one to whom we will direct our call and He is the only one who will be able to do something for us. So, it is essential that we face the truth of the Scriptures that the Church is communicating to us in a spirit of determination and obedience for our own salvation. It is important for us to build our faith in the Lord risen from the dead so that we may become people of good heart, ready to love, to forgive and to surrender ourselves totally to the Lord. Otherwise, if we don't build our faith on the resurrection of the Lord, we will be members in name only of the Church and we will not be transformed. We will be like those who don't know the Lord and act in a very worldly manner in everything. The faith built in the Risen Lord is a blessing for our own lives because the passion, the death and the resurrection of the Lord is being actualized in our lives every day. It is a school dedicated to us so that we may learn how to handle things that are painful and still maintain our peace. In many parts of the world and in many relationships, you still can witness the presence of Judas who continues to betray. There are still many false accusations and condemnations that are made, and there are still many crosses of life that are trying to scare many of us. However, the example that Jesus has given us through His Passion and Resurrection is enough for us to take courage and learn from. He has shown us how to forgive those who might betray and offend us. He has given us an example on how to trust the Father and put everything into His hands. In this way, He is a Shepherd, a Leader who cares about us so that we don't get lost and fall victim to all the madness that is happening in the world. God always prevails. Place your full trust in Him.

God Is Present In The Heart Of Everyone

Indeed, God is present in the heart of every human being. Though in this world of today, we will be scandalized by the way some people treat others, we may tend to believe that God is not present in their hearts. God is there in the heart of every human person. We have the choice to hear or to reject His voice whenever we do something. There will always be these situations where some groups of people, because of their education at home or because of the confusion they carry, may believe that God did not create one human being. Therefore, based on that lie in their head, they will always act in a way that shows disrespect and mistreatment to others by the evil words they say to them and by the continuous attack they make toward those particular persons. The truth is that we all have one Father. And Praised be the Lord, the Father is the one who unites us despite the illusion many human beings may have in their heads. We are supposed to live together in harmony and in peace. We are living in a world where still today, we realize that human beings do not know how to treat their brother. Beautiful statement about love and hospitality can be said easily, but it becomes more difficult to love especially when we are challenged by the presence of a person who is different. When God is recognized as important in the life of a person, it won't be a problem for that person to love and to welcome anyone, particularly if both belong to the same Catholic religion. Again, if faith is important in the life of someone, that person will be transformed to the point that when he welcomes another, he will do it as if he was welcoming Jesus. The Lord Jesus is the Son of the Father who comes to remind us that we are all part of the flock of whom He is shepherd. We all have one shepherd and we, the sheep, must hear his voice. He is telling us not to be discouraged by those who want to put us down. He wants us to remain firm and confident in the face of all difficulties that we may encounter in our lives. Only this way will we build relationships between us by hearing the voice of the Lord calling us for unity and peace. Only in the Lord God, can a person bring peace to another one. Only with the Help of the Lord will we choose to offer the other cheek instead of striking back. As the Lord says, not everyone has faith. Indeed, there are people who are out there with bad intentions. Sometimes, they will fabricate false accusations just to attack you even though you never open your mouth to say anything to them. As believers of the Lord, we have to be aware of that so that we don't get totally surprised when it occurs. Since we are made in His image it stands to reason that we have a spiritual dimension to us. We need to maintain this divine aspect of our being by educating our heart with spiritual and divine food that will keep us always in the path of the Lord. By educating ourselves, our love for the other will never stumble even though we may have good and bad moments. That is the reason why the Lord says: "My sheep hear my voice". The Love of God is the engine that keeps the world alive. It is this generosity of the Lord upon us and His role model which gives us desire and strength to love others and to be good to them. The love of God is without comparison particularly when we see that, despite our sinful nature, the Lord trusts us and is very patient with us. If we were able to love others as does the Lord God, we would resolve many problems in our world. The difficulty that sometimes discourages and surprises many of us is that we all talk about love but only with God can we really live it. We all can learn from God in order to love without counting and without any hypocrisy. We see that there are others who don't know how to love. The latter complicate life by being negative wherever they go. They are either difficult to please because they are never satisfied or they are too demanding. Because of this, it is important for us to keep our hearts open to the Lord in order to avoid being angry people. The Lord can teach us how to love. He can give us the tools we are missing in our being in order for us not to leave this world without making the effort to love. When we reach that level of love, there will be no malice, no suspicion nor anger within ourselves rather the awareness of being a human being who can only love through the help of the Lord. It is the only way to be a light in the world and from there we will be able to present the other cheek instead of striking back.

THE ASCENSION OF THE LORD, A SIGN OF BLESSINGS UPON US

THE LORD THROUGH HIS RESURRECTION has brought a lot of blessings upon us so that we may experience life in its fullness. One of these gifts that we have received is the gift of faith: "Blessed are those who believe without seeing". It is an important thing for us to have in this world of today. With everything going on in the world and with multiple issues that we have witnessed lately, our only comfort is faith. It is important for us parents to do what it takes in order to embrace the Catholic faith with joy, trust and obedience because there resides the joy of our future particularly through our children. If we fail to support the faith, we will be the cause of our own failure and our own misery. The reality is that our children watch everything we do. If we embrace the faith with devotion, respect and trust, the chance is better for our children to emulate us. We set the stage. Whenever they have a problem, they will know where to go to find strength. In addition, when they are away from us in another state or country, there is no need to be worried because we know that these values are embedded along with the principles of the Catholic faith. Indeed, when a parent knows that his son or daughter who is living abroad or in another state, attends Mass regularly and has no problems whatsoever with the faith, this brings security and contentment to the family. What could make you happier than to know that your children and grandchildren are following the faith? Many families are comfortable to know that their children go to Church and are involved in the community where they belong. We have to know how to prepare our happiness for the future by giving the right example to the children to emulate and be their leader in the faith. If as parents, we have issues with the faith, we need to resolve them by submitting our pride to the authority of the Gospel. We all have the faculties and we all are intelligent. Those who have made the effort to believe, they have done it not because they don't have the faculties, not because they are not intelligent, but because they have understood that, throughout the centuries for over two thousand years, many millions of souls believed in God. They have followed Him and they never questioned anything about the faith. It is not for us to rebel against the truth of the Scriptures. We have to resolve these problems by making sacrifices in thinking first about the role model we have to assume so that the children may learn from us. The difficulty is that if the children are witnessing from us a combative attitude toward the truth of the faith, we may contribute to their confusions and their indecisions. If that is what is happening, it is urgent to come to the Lord and ask Him to bless us with the gift of faith so that we may understand that the faith is not an invention of the Church, nor a caprice of a messenger but a blessing whose purpose is to help us be part of God's Kingdom. We should never reject the faith because of our weaknesses and our failures. If we have problems about being faithful to the Lord in a manner that does not allow us to receive the Eucharist or confession, it is better to turn to the Lord and ask Him to help us examine our conscience and change our lives. It is more beneficial to recognize that we have sinned and, through patience, we may some day change our lives. There is no point to diminish the truth of the faith and to fall into the habit of having our personal perceptions and interpretations of the Scriptures. The faith cannot be practiced through our personal perceptions because it is not the faith of the pope nor a bishop nor a priest. It is the faith given to us by Jesus Christ risen from the dead and ascended into Heaven. It is our heritage. The faith will teach us many things that will allow us to be less judgmental. During the Passion of the Lord, we have learned how to love, how to forgive and how to put everything into the hands of God. We have learned how to really live our lives which are filled with challenges and difficulties. All of this means that the true life is in the Lord because He has given us the tools we need to face the problems we may encounter in our lives. Now that He has ascended to the Father, He reminds us that we all who follow Him in the same path that He has shown us, will also ascend into Heaven. However, we have to experience the reality of the cross. There is no life without the cross. To live in the Lord means to be obedient to His word through the Church. When a person does his best to remain faithful to the faith, despite its challenges, the heart obtains a degree of consolation. The Lord is not asking things that are impossible to do. He just wants from us a humble attitude that can accept what He is saying for our own salvation. It is not easy to believe, because we have to give up our own pride. It means that humility is the first step for a person to have faith. Without this effort, everything that the messenger of the Lord will present to us will be considered as an insult, a lack of respect and lack of care. Faith will come in the hearts of those who are humble and are open to learn. If we are full with confusion from the enemy, we will travel around looking for happiness and we will never find it. Lies cannot give us happiness. They can give us some satisfaction but it is a temporary cover-up, something that is not real and deep. As we grow in our spiritual journey, we discover that the joy of the Lord in our lives is a blessing where we all must bring our cooperation in order to reach it. Let us open our hearts and minds to understand that, in this world, only God matters. Let every heart fully place his/her trust in the Lord.

THE LORD'S FORGIVENESS IS
AN ACT OF LOVE FOR US

To RECEIVE THE GIFT OF forgiveness from someone to whom you have been ungrateful and whom you have offended is something beyond comparison. It consoles one's heart and allows a person to feel delivered from a heavy burden. When the Lord forgives us, He does it with a sincerity of heart and everything becomes new. He gives us a chance to start over. He does not want us to be victims of sin, He gives us the grace of forgiveness and He teaches us how to forgive those who hurt us. If we are believers and can place our trust in the Lord, we can follow the Lord's example by giving a second chance to whoever has offended us. If God is able to forgive us for our sins, then we should be open to forgive people who have done us wrong; it is of God's blessings and we should learn to practice it and often. We should do whatever it takes for us to forgive others even if it hurts; otherwise, we will never experience God's peace in our heart. When we choose not to forgive others, we are just punishing ourselves. It is a form of enslavement which forbids freedom and this can hurt us in the long run. We find people who say that he or she would risk his/her life for you. This is not credible inasmuch as human statements are like hot air. It is forever changing. Jesus is a man of one word. His yes is yes; we can always count on Him. Who else in this world would live with you and would never cause you a headache nor betray you? In this day and age, many people will say to one another "I love you". But, in reality, what does such a statement truly mean in our daily lives? When two people meet for the first time, there is always this chemistry that brings them together like a magnet; sometimes they associate it with a gift coming from God. With that understanding and acceptance, they become ecstatic to have met that person. Depravation of sleep occurs. There is the refusal to eat because they have so much joy of encountering the "person of their dream". Young people living at home spend countless hours on the phone, texting or emailing rather than participating in the many family activities such as dinner, prayer or sitting together. But one should never invest too quickly in a relationship because there may be a number of things that one will not be able to see if one gets too emotionally involved. It is always prudent and wise to take the time and discover who the person is before thinking about marriage. If it is really a gift from God, it should be able to last forever without any real damage to the foundation and both in good and in bad times. The problem is that when there is no prudence and wisdom, one can make mistakes by assuming something that is not remotely reciprocated and since there is blindness, one enters into the relationship with a lot of expectations. Relationships can be challenged, when submerged characteristics emerge. Many relationships have been attacked in that way, because they went into it with too many expectations and less wisdom and prudence. In that particular setting, sooner or later, the hurtful wrath arises. When reality finally arrives, one starts seeing things clearly, things that were already there but that he/she could not see before. Then relationships, once loving couples, enter into continual fighting with one another, outdoing the other with words that hurt. The challenge is that these individuals become so involved in the struggle to win that they cannot forgive each other to begin a new and wholesome relationship. The truth is that in a relationship where people cannot forgive each other it can and will lead to disaster, pain and more hurt. The Lord God knows how to forgive and His forgiveness is so precious that whoever receives it becomes a new creature totally renewed. We have to give people the chance to start over, if the encounter was really a gift from God. There may be relationships that were not meant to be. Nevertheless, when we try to do our will instead of following God's will, the result will be that we spend our entire life in interminable conflicts. It is important to understand that not every person you meet can and should be your spouse or your friend for the reason that there are people the Lord has put in your path only for a moment. It means that you can help them if they have problems but it does not mean that they have to be your spouse or your friend. Problems you encounter in your courtship, if they are not resolved before marriage, will remain in the entire relationship like extra baggage. It is important to know that when a relationship of courtship is rocky where there are many problems, and if you are not strong enough to accept the challenges, it is wise not to choose the path of marriage with that particular person. It is better to stop the relationship before the marriage rather than to go through it with the illusions that it will change later. Problems you see in the courtship normally remain the same if you marry, they never change. So, understand that if you discover that you have made mistakes, before they become unmanageable, go to confession and the Lords' forgiveness will help you to start anew.

The Identity Of Christ In Our Lives Is A Challenge

As believers, we all know who Jesus is and what He has done for us in coming into the world. However, in our private life, his identity varies in accordance with what we attribute to be his blessings upon us. When things are going well, we know without any doubt that He is the one who gives us strength to keep going and being alive in a world filled with problems. Indeed, without the Lord, where would we be? Many of us have a lot to say regarding the many blessings we have received from the Lord. We have been blessed by the Lord in many ways: the fact that we know He is there for us at any time, the fact that we know He will never abandon us and the fact that we know He forgives us when we are sorry for our sins are things that give us joy. We need not to mired in the many trials we may go through in our lives. It is important to know that the Lord is there with us because, as human beings, we will always be challenged by the realities of life. They may come from our children, from our family members, from our friends, and from the people we love. They may also arise from our mortal bodies where we have to deal with some health issues. It means that we will always have a situation which requires our trust and hope. In that particular moment, we will have to place ourselves on our bended knees to talk to the Lord. There, out of frustration and pride, not willing to accept the problems that are causing us pain, we may try to disregard the presence of the Lord. We may even try to blame Him for our misery and not trust Him fully. One of the good virtues we should have in these particular situations is to be in a constant attitude of prayer with the purpose of placing everything into the hands of the Lord. We should have the desire to pray so that we may not fall into temptations and despair. The temptation that the Church is mentioning here is at all levels: flesh, pride, arrogance, suspicion and sensitivity. As believers, we have to educate ourselves in our faith so that we know how to utilize those good habits we possess and gather them all together in the daily activities of our life. Those talents can cause us more pain and more problems if we don't know how to channel them in our relationship with one another. It is important to be sensitive, but frequent suffering and frequent conflicts may occur if we can't balance good listening when we are communicating with others. The Christian life is a challenge. It is a daily task that requires much patience and humility and constant nurturing. Sometimes, in the face of something we consider to be an assault, we may be tempted to use force and violence to show that we are the dominant being since especially we are living in a world that rewards the strength through violence and aggression. However, in the spiritual world of Jesus, we show our strength by presenting the other cheek. As followers of the Lord, we cannot forget these values which make us members of the Catholic Church. Nevertheless, there is another world where, in the face of every attack either from another person or from life itself through illness or other problems, we have to ponder over this question of Jesus: "Who do you say that I am"? If He is the one who reminds us about the other cheek, then we must always try to let Him provide the answer to someone who is rude to us. We will always see His presence in our daily difficulties of life. We will always see Him walking beside us and we should never have any fear nor have any reason to use violence. Jesus brings us to the different levels in life, with the blessed guidance of the Holy Spirit we can find our peace, peace among ourselves and for others.

FREEDOM IS ONE OF THE MOST PRECIOUS GIFTS GIVEN TO US BY THE LORD

EACH ONE OF US HAS moments when we have to make decisions. At times, these decisions have been painstaking, yet other times the decisions have given us the opportunity for wisdom and the knowledge to be prudent. Others have ruined the trajectory of our lives in destructive force. If we turn to the Lord and learn from Him, we can change our lives and mend the bad decisions that we have made. Only by reforming our lives in the Lord can we turn a disastrous situation or relationship into something that gives dignity to our persona. Otherwise, we will spend the rest of our lives in misery, conflicts and belittlement from life itself. It means that every decision we make can contribute to our happiness or lead us to problems, frustration and even sufferings. Some of us will learn in a very obedient manner because we will listen to the Lord who speaks to us via friends, parents, Church or circumstances of life. Others will never learn because they choose not to listen. When we decide not to listen because we delude ourselves, our future can be so disastrous that only a divine intervention can bring us back to recovery. It is important to know how to listen in this life because if there is a fire that is kindled and we cannot perceive it, it means that the problem is with us and within us. Because of the love we should have for ourselves, when situations like that occur, we have to do our best to listen to those who have been successful in life and learn from them. It is important to know how and when and even where to give the best to ourselves in order to succeed. We were not created to fail. Failure is the result of bad decisions (If you never touch drugs you will never get addicted to it). But if we become free in the Lord, it won't be a problem for us to learn even from a child. The human being is a mystery that no one can really understand in a logical manner. We are the product of the love of the Lord. It is the same thing as the universe. As many of us place technology first, we may presumably think that we understand everything about human beings, about the universe and about who we are. There is no human science available yet that can really define the human person in terms of its multiple components that make him/her a person. Only in faith can we have a glimpse of what the human person is. This does not mean that faith and reason cannot work together. This intervention is not trying to deny the role of reason in the understanding of the universe. On the contrary, it is saying that faith allows people to have reservations about many elements of our existence. It is extremely essential for a person to have faith. One of our downfalls in this world is that there are too many secular approaches about the identity of man and we fail to accept the presence and the existence of a divine authority. Because of our pride, we think that we know everything while there are many things that we don't know and that we will never know because we are just mortal people. In other words, we are so limited by the confines of our mortal capacity that we must choose the path of humility. That is the reason why it is important to have faith which allows us not to be extremist people either on the left as well as on the right. True Faith allows people to have balance in their judgment and to walk always with the Church. When the true faith is not present in the life of a person, there is a tendency to follow ideologies and instead of following the Lord, we prefer to go with a particular person or belief. And if the elements of that particular ideology are not encountered in a leader of a particular community, that leader is subject to many false accusations. The faith is the fruit of our freedom. It gives us the possibility to be humble knowing that there are many things that we cannot comprehend: however, being aware of the marvels of the Lord, we make room to convey all those inexplicable realities to Him who has power to create life, the universe and everything that is in it. We have been given the gift of freedom. We are free either to walk with the faith or to reject it. There are consequences for whatever decisions we will make. Only based on that mystery, freedom can become for everyone one of the most precious gifts from the Lord. Freedom in this sense should be interpreted as courage and the decision to embrace and do something that is beneficial for oneself. The freedom to follow the challenges of the Catholic faith is the fruit of an internal reflection upon something that is difficult. However, we decide to follow without any fear knowing that it is the best thing to do. Our sense of freedom should be educated so that we may always choose the best for us in all things. But note that the Lord in His wisdom and limitless blessings stirs us. He speaks to us. He sometimes shakes and awakens us to follow him. We do have the choice either to heed His words or not. Understand, however, that there is a consequence for whatever one we decide to follow.

If We Are True Believers, We Must Be People Of Reconciliation

THERE IS A PRICE TO pay for the one who wants to become a disciple of the Lord. This statement applies to everyone regardless of the capacity in which he/she decides to serve the Lord either as a married or a single person. We all are called to be a disciple of the Lord. This is a task that concerns us all as Catholics: to go and be a messenger for the Lord by being a role model or spreading the good news wherever we are. If we are Catholics and we work in a place that is anti-Catholic, it becomes more difficult for us to bear witness: however, we should not be afraid to say the truth. We are called to contribute to the coming of the Kingdom in the way we live our lives with hope. If we are people who have hope, we will always be joyful because hope is the source of our joy. If we are going through some tribulations we will be challenged, tested in the seeming absence of hope. If we believe that we shall see the goodness of the Lord in the land of the living, it provides us joy and will facilitate our communication with other people. At times, when people are under the strain of the rigors of life and hope is deficient, the result can be painful. Thus, any type of verbal communication can become suspicious and can be a source of conflict. If we have distractions coming from the trials of life, we are invited to put all of them in the hands of the Lord and we must do this with the utmost reverence for the power and grace that reside in the Lord. We will be in a better attitude to speak to the members of our family and our friends. The problem is that when there is no spiritual strength within us in the middle of our problems, we tend to blame others for what is happening in our lives. Anything that is simple becomes an exaggerated issue pushing us to create painful situations for no good reason. Nevertheless, the conversion of the heart is a message that is sent to everyone so that the Kingdom of God may come into the world through everything that brings unity and peace. It requires poverty and simplicity of the heart to be the missionary Jesus expects from us. Indeed, life is at the same time simple and complicated. The way we live our faith on earth will have an impact on others which will allow them to join the faith and follow the Lord. If our faith is not strong, we will always remain in the emotional level where we become so egotistical that we forget about the needs of others and we put more emphasis on our desires. Is it not the reason why the relationship of two immature people, whether it be spousal or friendly, not work, because God's presence is not felt? The problem is that maturity is the key for a healthy relationship. When people know what they want and when they have reached the level of maturity in their lives through the faith in the Lord, peace is felt. They become lambs of God who are there only to share peace, love and grace. We all have to work hard in order to reach that maturity level when mutual respect can become the agenda in the relationship. We can only reach that level through prayer, meditation, humility, and desire for unity. It is important also to understand that this maturity does not go with the age of a person but rather with experience of intimacy in the Lord and the kind of life we want to experience while we are still breathing. It is a continuous path of resurrection where we put away the old world in our lives and choose the new one when we know that the Lord is waiting for us. This is where we are not only followers of the Lord but we will accept to carry in our body the mark of the sufferings of Christ; we will not be discouraged in the face of persecutions and contradictions because we are following Jesus who also went through them. If Jesus who is God went through persecutions and difficulties of all kinds, we ought to be very thankful and desire that the crosses we bear are all of God's gifts, sharing and desiring. If we can, feeling the presence of Jesus at times can be so intense that tears can flow from our eyes. This should be our longing in life. "May your love be upon us, O Lord as we put our trust in you" Ps. 33.

WE ALL HAVE BEEN
BLESSED BY THE LORD

THE BLESSINGS OF THE LORD in our lives are without comparison. They are the source of our peace and joy because they give us the desire and the strength to always move forward removing distractions and other confusions in living a good life. These blessings of the Lord are etched in our hearts and from time to time we are called to visit and meditate upon them in order for us to experience the love of God in our lives. Such blessings allow us to be vibrant and successful in all the trials we encounter. Indeed, no difficulties of life are greatly desired; however, with the Lord's blessings, we learn how to cope with them. It means it is important for us to learn how to deal with all kinds of hardships in our lives. It is essential that we find a way to accept difficulties such as death in our own family or from any other crisis in life. Faith is the key. If we remain close to the Lord through His Church, it will be easier for us to understand the dynamics of everything that occurs in our lives. Praying can be an ordeal when one is hurt and when one gets angry at God. If we discover that God has not answered our prayers as we think He ought to, we tend to abandon him. How can faith be maintained when prayers have not been answered the way that fits us? Our injured senses are not the end, they are a means to include God even more. God is the one who gives us life and He is the one who takes it away. He takes it away not because He wants to cause us pain. He takes it away because no one is eternal in this world. Each of us has a time to be born and a time to die. We should never forget this reality whenever one of our family members departs from this life and not to question God about that loss. We belong to Him. Faith is a process. We have to be willing to have it so that we may be ready for the next trial in the family. In the process, the evil one constantly brings us to a trap. Indeed, there will be other ensnarements for there is no life in this world without trials. Whenever it comes, as people of faith, we will have to say: I am the handmaid of the Lord, may it be done to me according to your will. Faith is God's gift to us and a very good way to cope with trials and anxieties is to always turn to the Lord. Not only will it bring joy in our hearts, it will also allow us to pray for the one who has departed and to give comfort and consolation to the ones who have been left on earth to grieve. This is the way that we will get our mission accomplished. These blessings of consolation are already present in our hearts, we have to know how to nourish this wealth so that whenever we are confronted by a trial, big or small, we must surrender to God and put everything into His hands. This is a way to show our appreciation to God and also our love for the person who dies because faith allows us to pray for his soul and for his eternal rest. Yes indeed, we are humans, it is normal to have pain but we are Christians; we must have faith so that we accept situations no matter how painful they are. Acceptance with dignity is what we pray to God for. When we maintain our faith and continue to worship God even though we experience the pain of death, we will gain more peace because every time we get close to God, it gives us an opportunity to pray to God for that particular deceased member forgetting our own pains. But if we are separated from God, when prayers cannot be summoned, it means that we are missing many opportunities, i.e. to pray for our loved ones who died. In fact, anyone who dies needs prayer. Our responsibilities here on earth are to pray for the ones who died. We should speak to God more often. Because of the love we have for those who died, we cannot separate ourselves from God. If not us, who would pray for them?

We cannot stop coming to Church where we find our daily bread. If not, where else can we go? The Lord has been always good to us. He will never tire listening to us and to care about us. However, it is surprising to see man's lukewarm reaction toward the goodness of the Lord in his/her life. The blessings of the Lord cannot be interpreted in the realm of our own desires. The will of the Lord must come first.

Our prayerful perception affects our attitudes and behaviors towards others. It affects how we accept our challenges and our lives with our limitations. If our heart is pure and only centered in God, the world we live in can be different.

THE PRESENCE OF THE
LORD IN OUR LIVES

INDEED, THE LORD HAS ALWAYS been present in our lives. From the beginning of creation until today, He has not ceased to manifest Himself and His love for us so that we may be protected from all types of danger. In this life, there are all kinds of situations that can cause us sadness, violence, anger and frustration, because of our corrupt nature. Anyone of us can fall in any of them and be a victim of one of these challenges in life. When we see a person beset with problems, we should never assume that this would never happen to us. We should take it to heart as a reminder that we may be the next one. This is inevitable for as we live in this world we are not exempt from them. While living in this world, sooner or later, we will have to face some challenges. They may be very frightening and sometimes we can fall into despair. Sometimes, it has nothing to do with us being good or bad, it is just a question of being a mortal person and we cannot escape from them. That is the reason why the presence of the Lord is so essential in our lives. We must do whatever we can in order to seek him, to look for him and to call upon Him at every instant of our life. The Lord should be in our minds, on our lips, in our hearts constantly so that we may be ready for the day of trials. Without the grace of the Spirit, we don't see what the Lord has prepared for us in the different and various activities of our daily life. Everything that brings a challenge will be taken as a heavy burden and a punishment. Many times, when we experience the dark moments where either our children or other members of our families have fallen, doubts occur instead of trying to feel the presence of the Lord in this particular situation. Anger and accusations

196

are directed to the Lord. What have I done wrong? We expect exemption because we consider ourselves righteous, never having wronged anyone and we justify things by stating all the litanies of our goodness. Rationalization seeps in. But as Catholic believers, we must open our hearts to the Lord during moments of difficulties. God always speaks to us and, whenever He speaks, He gives us a message that we need to hear and that we need to see. If we close our hearts and minds to Him, we wallow in our corruption and immaturity, thus lose hope. If we are not willing to see the presence of the Lord in everything that happens to us we will never grow spiritually and, when there is no spiritual growth in our lives, we stagnate. The Lord is so marvelous, so mysterious, so compassionate that He would use any means in this world to talk to us or to teach us something that may appear negative to us. If we don't have a relationship with God we are left with deception, suffering and self destruction. The Lord manifests Himself to us for what He has to say is important during good times, and even during undesirable times. A person who is not spiritual doesn't accept the teachings of God's spirit. He thinks they're nonsense (Cor. 2, 14). It is a mystery that we cannot comprehend without the gift of faith. Our life is not as simple as we may think. We are connected to many spiritual realities that are visible and invisible. The faith brings something so important to us that whoever has a strong faith will never panic whenever he is in the middle of a difficulty or a crisis. The faith also gives us another understanding of our own life. We are dust and to dust we will return. The meaning of our life exists only in the Lord, away from Him, we can just be mistaken and fall into pride and false judgment. If anyone has doubt about his faith, that person should pray to the Lord in order to receive this gift. It is so important for us to build our lives on spiritual things because, in the end, God is the only wealth we will be able to carry with us. At the end of our earthly life, when it's the last time we close our eyes and that we are taking the last breath, the name of God will be the only possession we will carry with us, nothing else. Either we will say: Lord, have mercy on me or Lord help me or Lord forgive me. Because of our faith, in our worship or our prayer before God, the future is always full of hope because we can see His presence throughout these crises and difficulties. So, we must remain in the Lord. The first step is humility. Humility is the basis to see the Hands of God, helping us, talking to us, consoling us or inviting us to a higher level of spiritual life. The Lord can speak to us through people we meet. Three things remain: faith, hope and love. But the best one is love: love for God and for our neighbor.

THE LORD GIVES LIFE TO MAN

SOMETIMES PEOPLE HAVE AN ERRONEOUS image of God, perceiving Him as a distant God who lives in Heaven and intervenes in our lives only to punish or to judge us. Gn: 18, 20-32 provides another aspect of God's identity. He graciously accepted a bargain with Abraham with the purpose of provoking a conversion of heart and to allow those who are willing to follow Him obtain salvation. God does not wish anyone to be lost neither does he chastise His people. He does not even wish that any of His children should be oppressed or punished. God says: "if you want to come after me, you must deny yourself and carry your cross". Indeed, the Lord wants us all to be saved and while we are on earth, He wants us to experience His yoke. His yoke is joy and one that can bring salvation. When we live in the Lord all our burdens become lighter. God consoles us with encouragement saying to us: "Come to me all who labor and are heavy burden and I will give you rest (Mt. 11, 28)". With the Lord, even though life can be unbearable and sometimes painful, we can learn how to endure sufferings and maintain hope. But if we don't have an intimacy with the Lord, it will be difficult to realize God's love in our lives and such ingratitude leads us to more difficulties. Without prayers, it will be impossible to go through life's calamities without anxieties. It is extremely important for us to allow God to know our requests, to maintain our faith and to be loyal to the Church and its teachings. It is God's dwelling. It is the place where the Lord wants us to establish partnership with Him. With that, our lives can be more joyful so that we may contribute to our own happiness. Everyone is responsible for his / her own fate regarding salvation; it is based on this simple premise: We can continue to exist but without the Lord we can do nothing. We will attain a spiritual bliss when we perceive his gifts: for us to experience His love and the realization that He is everything and everywhere thus creating a partnership with Him. He gives us the Eucharist, He gives us the gift of confession, He gives us the Scriptures and the sacraments, all the devotions that are in the Church so that we may live in peace and under His grace. He gives us the strength to carry and helps in our crosses, anxieties, He allows us to obtain forgiveness but expects us to forgive those who have offended us. If we truly desire and seek God's partnership, then we should work together for a common purpose. We will ask Him for His blessings, blessings that we truly need as in charity, humility and acceptance. The Lord is not far away from us when we realize that He is our bedrock and when we are in harmony with Him. We can pray for His blessings so that we may remain faithful and obedient in everything we do with our life. If we nurture our faith on a daily basis, through prayers, it can have this form of partnership with the Lord. As a believer, if a member of your family dies, pray for him/her in the spirit of solidarity as Jesus died and rose from the dead, masses and devotions help. Being angry and questioning God is not following His will. One will grieve after death but God will help during these moments. Accepting death as part of our life on earth would alleviate feelings of anger and frustrations. Accept that our lives on earth end. One's life is brief and at any given moment it ends. Continue to turn to the Lord begging for His Mercy and counting on His strength to hold us in His Arms. In Jesus, we find Abraham, the father of faith. Coming to Church, visiting the Blessed Sacrament, and asking the Holy Spirit for wisdom and fortitude with our hearts are good practices. It is essential that the faith we have should be an obedient and mature faith where humility and love for God are the fundamentals. When the Lord speaks, the only thing we should say is the following: "Here I am Lord, I come to do your will". It is the kind of faith when we really become children of God, and God is considered to be our Father. The more we become children of God, the more we feel the urgency to love God above all with all our hearts and with all our strength. We will discover that such is all we need in our mortal life. In the meantime, let us keep and nurture living in God's blessed, refreshing and tender love.

HEAVEN IS THE GOAL
OF ALL CHRISTIANS

WE WILL ALL BE ONE in Christ the moment we acquiesce to live in love. As St. Paul recalls in 1Cor. 12: 31-13:2 "If I give away all that I possess, piece by piece, and if I even let them take my body to burn it, but am without love, it will do me no good whatever". In addition, God is love and whoever believes in this love that Jesus has come to reveal to us will contribute to a redeemed world that we all long for. It is important to work hard, to be honest and to have a strong desire in gaining the grace of God through the efficiency of prayers and good works. The Lord in creating the world gives that instruction to Adam in Gn 3: 17 "You will have to work hard and sweat to make the soil produce anything until you go back to the soil from which you were formed". This means that by working hard, a person can become successful in life but that success is not eternal life, rather it is the consequence of Adam's disobedience. The benefits are good only as a response to the needs of one's earthly life as a mortal being. It is not eternal joy. While money is important to one's existence, it is only a means, for many things depend on having it. We rely on it to pay for the necessary aspects of life such as food and shelter. We need it to help our own parish to survive. Without it, it would be disheartening for many of us and for our Church. Being successful and having money are gifts from the Lord to us with the purpose of helping the unfortunate but they do not constitute complete happiness. Only Jesus can bring true joy to each and every one of us. Therefore, there is no need for envy if and when a brother or a sister or a neighbor is more successful than the rest of us. If someone has had the opportunity to have a good or better job and has earned more successfully, we must render praise and thanksgiving to the Lord. Being envious is the devil's allure. Taking what the Lord has not given us offends Him. We can only pray that the success of an individual can be shared by the few who don't have anything. It is evangelical to encourage the successful to practice charity toward those who are in need. This can be done either by providing opportunities when the jobless can't find a job and get paid living wages demonstrating the skills needed. It is also helpful and fundamental to create an atmosphere where one can find his/her self-worth and take pride in one's contributions without feeling like the recipient of a hand-out, because each human person is a valuable asset for the success of the community in which we live. When we prefer not to work and choose receiving, the consequences are denying our dignity and denying the Lord's gift to Adam and to us. Other systems of government, like the communist system, refuse to live by God's words and suggest that one can forcefully take away the temporal wealth of a person and share it with others. It has been tried for years. However, the success of such governments is from little to none. The logic is this: if a society does not promote work ethics, there will be no productivity. And if one takes out of the big box one has, there will be a time when emptiness surfaces and there is no going back. This is not what Jesus would do. During His mission, He was also confronted with this kind of suggestion, when a man in the crowd said to Him: Master, tell my brother to give me a share of our inheritance", He responded to the other brother: "Who appointed me to be your judge or the arbitrator of your claims (Lk 12: 13-21). By responding that way, Jesus is not ignoring the need of the less fortunate nor promoting injustice in the world. On the contrary, He is reminding us that wealth can be deceptive if one tries to make of it the only source of peace and joy. On the other hand, if Jesus does not promote such ideology, it means that it does not belong to us to adopt such manners to resolve the problems of the poor. If people think that they are cursed because materially they don't have that much, it can only lead to pain, jealousy and turmoil. Being rich should not merely account for one's material possessions. Our main concern should only be the presence of God: to love Him above all, to be humble and meek. He may lead all to Heaven. Today let us invite the Lord to take you and me in His Hands to deliver us from the wiles of the devil. With this, we pray to the Holy Spirit to strengthen us and provide us with the wisdom we need during our earthly journey.

Poverty Can Be A Source Of Corruption

DURING DIFFICULT TIMES, WHEN THERE is lack of money to sustain the family or whenever a myriad of problems occur thus causing us a lot of pain, Christians are encouraged to resort to things that are truly essential for spiritual and psychological growth. Eyes should be fixed on God, thought should be focused on God to whom we must listen in order to find an answer or a solution. We must understand that, when we experience difficulties, we are vulnerable, and prone to manipulation, even in the form of well-meant-advice. Such advice maybe will rescue us from the predicament in which we find ourselves or it can be ensnarement. The devil plays a big role in promising us alternatives that are clearly detrimental to our mental health and to our happiness if we decide to follow him. Because of our weaknesses, we don't see its destruction in the midst of roiling turmoil, i.e. losing one's boyfriend or girlfriend or going through economic crises or hardships. Turning to the Lord with strong faith can peacefully resolve these issues. The devil can tread through our minds and will start bargaining with us. He promises us heaven and earth. He does this so smoothly so as to present the rosiest picture, so we can't even fathom any negative. There are countries where poverty prevails; many citizens have lost their freedom because of it. Trusting in God is not the priority. Many have relied on the promises made to them by a self-proclaimed savior whose purpose is of building their own future; someone whom they believe will take care of them. It is a complex moment when one is undergoing hardships and cannot make sacrifices.

The sufferings to come may be more hurtful than the ones presently here now. It is important for us to be vigilant, always waiting for the Lord so that we may do the right things. We must also learn the lessons from the past, from other people or other societies that have already fallen into destruction. The misery is deeper than the one experienced before. Each of us is called to be another Good Samaritan. This calling means to do what we can to help the poor and to practice charity towards those who are in need. This has been a social practice since Jesus' time which has brought a lot of interest and scrutiny of many individuals such as the disciples of Jesus who grew indignant when they saw the costly perfume poured on the head of Jesus by that woman at the house of Simon the leper: "What is the point of such extravaganza. This could have been sold for a good price and the money given to the poor" (Mt. 26: 6-9). But material poverty can be a very difficult state of life. It is especially more difficult when there is no alternative in which one can find a solution. It is evangelical to eliminate poverty by establishing structures which can provide jobs for everyone. It is also essential that those who have the means to help the unfortunate may do so in a manner that allows them to get out of their poverty, to establish self worth. It is not something that obliges them to be dependent permanently. The problem is that, for many centuries, people who have claimed to be the saviors of the poor have always manipulated poverty to accomplish their ideologies. One needs to use discretion for those who are self proclaimed saviors. These saviors of the poor, who most of the time come from poor families, have created systems that allow them to be in control. They have enriched themselves while they tirelessly prohibit success to anyone else. With the system they have innovated, they have impeded many other citizens to express freedom thus using their talents in a free market enterprise. The tragedy is that those who advocate for the poor when they are in power are many times rich although they profess to be against the rich. They enjoy such accolades as being wealthy in their countries. Ironically, those who support their ways will remain poor. Jealousy? Perhaps manipulating the name of the poor to reach the level where they want to be is their practice. When one looks at reality, nothing is free. One may fill his/her belly with the food the government may provide. The question is this: "Does one have to lose his freedom and many other rights in order to be helped"? It is wise to look at Cuba, Venezuela,

Vietnam, North Korea and the rest in order to learn. It is easy to discover the madness that is behind all the generosity and the guise of helping the poor. There is a lack of freedom (freedom of expression, freedom of traveling or freedom of worshiping God). The rations, the dependence and the corruption are enough to teach us a lot of wisdom. The sad part of it is that many citizens of those countries have fallen into a trap and it is very difficult and even impossible for them to extricate themselves and attempt the pursuit of happiness. No other way exists. Another irony in that kind of system is that religion is considered to be a threat and therefore needs to be eliminated. Anyone who enters a church is considered to be an enemy of the system. So, people cannot express their love for God nor transmit the Christian values to their children. With all of that, it means we must continue to believe in the Lord and wait for Him to save us. Whenever we have a problem in whatever area of our life, we have to turn to God. He is the only one who has the means to resolve our problems and He will help us if we are a Good Samaritan. It is important to understand that the Good Samaritan is not God and he cannot take God's place. We will need to make sacrifices such as being patient. We should never trade off our rights and freedom for material help promised by those who claim to be friends or saviors of the poor. If we remain in the faith, we should never be afraid of the future. The world belongs to God and no one else. We have all the reasons to wait in hope, joy and confidence because we are God's children. To know how to wait means that we already possess the treasure we are looking for. The Lord is the one who gives us the strength to do it. When we obey Jesus and His commands, we surrender to God.[...."I was given a thorn in the flesh[...]. Three times I begged the Lord that this might leave me. He said to me: My grace is enough for you for in weakness, power reaches perfection. And so I willingly boast of my weaknesses instead, that the power of Christ may rest upon me" (2Cor. 12: 9).

WHO WILL BE SAVED?

IN AN ERA IN WHICH the entrance into the Kingdom of God has been re-vindicated as to the confusion of some believers, it is an irrelevant question to ask which deceased family members or friends will be saved. We cannot be privy as to the fate of the deceased. Those who claim to have ownership of sending people to Heaven say: I know where he/she is. He/she is with God. Indeed, this should be every believer's desire that loved ones enter God's Kingdom. However, Jesus invites us to enter through the narrow door. Many have the desire to enter but they would not be able to do so. The last will be first and the first will be last. No one really knows where the soul goes after death. Only God knows. He is the only who knows and who can decide one's destination after death. Our responsibility as friends and family members is to offer prayers to the Lord for the soul of that loved one. The Church's willingness to help us deal with the reality of salvation motivates us to intercede for our faithful departed. The daily Mass is always the good offering for the eternal rest of those gone before us. It is also a good offering for the ones who are survivors. We can instill the importance of prayer for our beloved deceased children and grand children for their health and their well being. To contribute to their salvation is by asking God to have mercy upon them. It is a consistent task because no one really knows the final destination, and not ever can we assume that the soul has reached Heaven. This thinking lessens the necessity of prayers which we should offer to God for the souls of our loved ones. It is not automatic that the soul reaches Heaven right away at the hour of death. Not everyone who dies goes to Heaven. Above else, we need to examine the kind of relationship we have with the Lord. Do we follow the commandments because of the love we have for the Lord or is it just the plain reason of fear of hell. What motivates our almsgiving? Is it for the glory of the Lord or for something else? Do we blame God for our problems? Are we angry at Him for our misfortunes? If a person dies in such a condition without any repentance, he/she cannot be where God is for the reason that there is no place for anger in Heaven. God is love and in Heaven there can be only love. St. Paul gives us some instructions on how to please God so that we may be able to be chosen by Him. He says: "My sons do not disdain the discipline of the Lord nor lose heart when he reproves you [....]. Endure your trials as the discipline of God. But God does so for our true profit, that we may share his holiness. At the time it is administered, all discipline seems a cause for grief and not for joy, but later it brings forth the fruit of peace and justice to those who are trained in its school" (He 12, 5-13). What is being said is that we have to do our best to serve the Lord and to help others with our whole heart, our whole strength and whole being. He will take care of the rest. The provisions that the Lord sends us such as our freedom are there for us to seek the truth in our everyday lives. We have the choice to walk in the path of the Kingdom after God's calling or to reject it as we submit to our beliefs and ideologies regarding the Lord's call. We are our own big players in our final destination. The Lord would rectify our thoughts and attitudes when we don't conform according to His plan of salvation. The door for salvation is a narrow door. Not many people want do what is required to go through. The narrow door opposes depravity. It is not a place of fun and games but a place where each one is given many crosses to bear and the reality is that every family has its own cross. It is a place where the burden of life can get very heavy and where freedom appears to be limited. It is a place where the believer is asked to forgive and to move forward in order to save and protect the bond of unity. The truth is that not many of us like this kind of road. While the narrow door is the path of salvation, we have been brought up to dislike it because it is uncomfortable and freedom cannot be enjoyed. Because of this perception, we avoid these situations. Relationships have been destroyed because of this way of thinking. The truth is that wherever we are, everything would not meet our expectations. We may not have the wisdom to see it at a glance, but after a while, clarity emerges. If we don't want to grow in a spiritual way, we will spend our life moving from friend to friend or spouse to spouse looking for the one who can offer us a perfect relationship. It is important to remember that everything we do is connected to the Kingdom. This is the main reason why it is important to allow God to make the decision. It is His sole decision whether to welcome his people in His Kingdom or not. Without God's decision, no one is allowed. It is one's birth right from the Lord received which we obtain through sanctifying grace. This particular grace is a blessing from the Lord, received during Mass when we celebrate the Eucharist. It occurs during the consecration when the bread turns to the Lord's body and the wine His blood. We are consistently reminded with: "Do this in memory of me" during the consecration.

The Importance Of The Eucharistic Meal

THE EUCHARISTIC MEAL THAT WE receive at Mass in the Catholic Church is Jesus' gift to us. It consists of the Lord's body and blood. It is a source and means of strength. It is our daily bread. Having this meal as we make our pilgrimage on earth, we as travelers, are guided by the Lord. This occurrence is possible if we are led by faith. Not just anyone can receive it; it is a grace and a privilege granted to those who prefer not to walk with the world. Some contemporary interpretations about the reception of the Eucharist put the emphasis on one's "rights". But, the Body of the Lord is destined for those who prefer to choose the narrow door so that they may be transformed by the Lord. All this requires placing one's trust in the Lord, in His scriptures and in His Church. Our hearts must recognize that the Lord is our spiritual leader in a world where confusion continues to lurk and challenge the faith of so many. It is truly tragic that there is a kind of prestige in being disobedient to the faith. Honor is bestowed onto who is intelligent and brilliant even if the belief in God is void. Then there are the official teachings of the Church in the sacraments and in the Ten Commandments. The above should govern our lives; one should not be confused about the truth of God. We are people who embrace the Catholic Faith, thus allowing us to be called Catholics. Anything else comes from ideologies which do not emanate from the narrow door but from the world. These discernments and insights are detrimental to one's faith. On the surface, such ideals appear exemplary. One's intelligence, material gifts, speech and talents are all from God. God prefers and chooses the humble and the lowly ones and those who accept the faith without any malice. In the eyes of God and of the faith, humility is the key for knowing, acting and expressing. Humility opens the door for more blessings coming from the Lord. To understand the dynamics of the narrow door, one should accept the faith the way it is. The created mind may spend time reading and praying the Magnificat. It is when Mary surrendered her wisdom and understanding totally to the will of God. The Magnificat, if prayed slowly and with fervor, is a great example of obedience and humility. Such has become a model of proclamation and expression of faith. There is only one way and that is to totally trust the Lord as we have learned in our Catholic teachings and practices. To say that I am a "liberal Catholic" does not fit in the concept of the narrow door. The progressive movement that is trying to impose its agenda in the Church may have such kind of statements and beliefs, however it applies to the principle of the complete surrender to the divine Master as stated in the first commandment. Jesus expressed this surrender during the last supper. He assumed divine humility by choosing a path of death to give us life. If we choose to follow Jesus, we cannot allow ourselves to have such a liberal mentality in the faith. Logically and philosophically, it does not make any sense to have such a belief. We either follow the Lord Jesus or we follow the devil. Jesus expresses it very clearly: Those who are not with me, are against me and anyone who does not help me gather is really scattering (Lk 11, 23). It means that if the beliefs we have are not helping the growth of the Catholic faith we are promoting divisions and there is no need for us to maintain something that is damaging the Church of Jesus Christ. So, we must be careful about the ideologies of those who are acting as the enemies of the faith and we have to seriously think about the consequences of some beliefs that are not part of the teachings of the Church to avoid the wrath of God in our lives.

WE SHOULD INCLUDE GOD IN
ALL THE EVENTS OF OUR LIVES

WHATEVER WE INTEND TO DO in this world, it is essential that we allow the Lord to be part of our plans. Any decision we make in regard to something that would transform our lives or our future, allow God to be the center of it. Should we move to a new apartment or to a new house, invite a priest to bless this new dwelling? As we seek for a much needed job and God provides for our request, the utmost gratitude is warranted. Such gratitude can be expressed by lighting a votive candle or offering a mass showing the Lord our appreciation. Whatever our status in life, be it single or currently involved in a relationship, we should not be flippant about cohabiting. Submit to God's blessing. Such a great and special move is the Lord's sole decision. Any believer guided by the Holy Spirit would beseech God's graces and blessings. Any major decision crucial to one's salvation requires the Lord's intervention. As a result, peace of heart and mind will follow. One way to receive divine graces is to surrender to God during the celebration of the Eucharist. In the same spirit, good examples are very important to one's offsprings and are helpful to one's community. God's presence with a strong faith in Him can help us get through ultimately to have access to His Kingdom. God's presence allows us to govern our behaviors without resorting to despair and to extreme attitudes in times when jobs are lost and spending is restricted. Such are the blessings given to those who put their trust in the Lord.

One who believes in the Lord acknowledges suffering as a part of living. With God's guidance and blessings, it's sufficient. Respecting life as stated in the commandments is a very important part of our daily activities.

Taking one's life and aborting a life is not of God or from God. Such an act is heinous and God does not approve of it. It is important to embrace the faith as we inherit it from the Apostles. It is fundamental for peace to be felt. As we posture ourselves as peace-loving, when the demands or rigors in life befall, calmness is seemingly impossible. If we choose to remain in the Catholic Church, let it be a full and complete adherence. Our ancestors, as our fathers Abraham and Job, never questioned God. The Lord blessed them, their family, and their generations abundantly. If we are to follow the Lord and His teachings, then we take this to heart and practice His words. As Catholics, being part-time or being liberal is not an option. God's words are what we live by to praise, to love, to obey and to worship Him. The Human person is one who is limited. God is infinite and has no limits. Our own destruction can take place if too much emphasis is on the world. Let us strive to remain obedient to our faith. Surrendering to the Lord God, who is love, is the best way. It is the best gift we can bestow upon our children and grandchildren. No one possesses obedience more than the blessed Virgin Mother who accepted everything without questioning. The Lord makes it very clear that having wisdom does not constitute a mindset of "pick and choose". It is the attitude of humility allowing God to be God and we are His people. At the wedding in Cana, Mary reminded us to do whatever Jesus tells us. Indeed the Eucharistic meal at Mass reminds us to worship God and to celebrate His marvels. Jesus allows us two gifts: understanding and discretion which we can utilize when uncertainty and skepticism occur. The Eucharist invites us to put away our pride and idiosyncrasies. To do this, we can accompany the Lord until the crucifixion. The means are by being obedient and humble to the words and the will of God. And if today you hear his voice, harden not your hearts. Battling the active mind can pollute our faith. It can bring us to lose faith and stick to our own beliefs then to rationalize their existence. The last decade brought forth many controversies regarding the Eucharist. Many have abandoned the idea that sins do exist. However, only this meal will satisfy the hungry heart while we continue the journey here on earth. What gladness it is to know that after death, there is a welcoming God who will extend His love because we have accepted His grace and His teachings. Also, the Holy Spirit has filled us with His gifts. Let us maintain a heart with overflowing goodness and blessings from God for each day has its own newness and blessings.

GOD'S FATHERLY GENEROSITY

CAN GOD FORGIVE EACH AND every sin we commit? God's faithful know that God is love and any one who expresses regret would be forgiven. Nevertheless, some are dubious about God's forgiveness. Some of us find it difficult to believe that a particular sin has been absolved by confession. Such unbelief grates on our minds. Our Catholic faith teaches us that no matter how grievous a sin can be, confessing it would release its hold. The act of contrition and the priest's absolution impart blessings and our hearts transformed to purity as in pure of heart. As we resolve not to commit the same sin a pure heart wells up in us. This provides a tool to resist future temptations. After the absolution, we must take it to heart that God has transformed the core of our being so as not to repeat the same transgression. It is the hardened heart that sees no change, progress and improvement may not result. God's grace calls for our utmost fulfillment. It is essential to realize that the Lord forgives. Due to the immensity of His love for us, there is no sin venial or mortal that the Lord would not forgive. Jesus lovingly absolved the woman caught in adultery, His compassion for Zaccheus and how He forgives Barnabas as He hung from His cross are examples of His love and His forgiveness. The story of the prodigal son is the perfect example of God the Father's generosity. As we choose to reconcile our hearts with the Lord asking Him for forgiveness, the Lord would never turn down anyone who comes to Him. It is one of our callings to think of other's needs before our own needs: to show the same compassion and care to the other person. As humans, we find difficult to forgive others' mistakes; animosity or vindictiveness is so much easier. It is a way of punishing another for his/her offense. We must not save anything of ourselves; give it back to God. The humble soul will offer to God everything thus allowing Him to guide with what is blessed and holy. With our holiness, we can attain justice in the relationships and there will not be any delusions. Through His presence, the Lord Jesus allows us to discover the fatherly generosity of God by welcoming us. Inviting Him with the full desire to modify our lifestyles or to change our hearts is our resolution. In forgiving us, the Lord forgets everything that we have done against Him. He allows us to start anew, giving us life. To experience God's love and forgiveness is electrifying: knowing that someone is always ready to forgive and embrace us. When God forgives us, we are no longer under the bondage of sin. We are free from what has impeded us to be at peace with the Lord. Indeed, whenever we sin, not only do we commit an offense to God, it also separates us from the Lord. It is important to reestablish trust which was lost. If there is a relationship between two individuals and disagreements ensue thus the inability for one of them to forget and forgive, this relationship can be in danger of annihilation. To be followers of Christ, we forget ourselves so as to forgive someone. The act of forgiveness is not always easy but is one of our inheritances to experience the peace of Jesus. It is God's will. If and when this is not possible, then it is essential that we call upon the Lord and ask Him for His help. He will give us the strength needed to get over it and to move on as we leave everything in His hands. Since the Lord is the only one who can forgive sins, make the changes that are all for God not for ourselves. It is wise for us to seek for His guidance and clarity, if not, the devil will intervene and God's love is denied. Our thoughts and prayers should only be centered on God's forgiveness and mercy. Why? This leads to a fruitful and peaceful life. It also promotes a blameless life. The enemy tempts and promotes separation. Our God encourages unity. The Lord rejoices whenever a sinner repents and whenever the lost is found. He brings joy, peace and love to those who repent. We are called upon to bring the same things to those around us who have recognized their wrongdoings and can express regret. God is the only reliable source of forgiveness and love. Let us try hard to emulate Him. Maintaining a good relationship requires a high degree of nurturing, cherishing, disciplining. However, all this is possible through God's guidance and love because only God elevates you above your humanity. And only humble souls can receive and communicate these qualities.

THE ROLE OF MONEY:
SYMBOL OR IDOL

SINCE JUDAS HAS CONTRIBUTED TO the fate of Jesus on the cross for 30 pieces of silver, money has become a source of confusion for human beings and of controversy to those who want to follow the Lord. Despite its important role in the life of the human person it has failed to bring happiness to the human heart. However, the mentality is that even though Judas could not find happiness obtained from the price as he sold Jesus, some people are convinced that money can change lives totally and bring comfort. Some would work hard and invest with the goal of having a good retirement, but death can surprise us and the enjoyment we expected remains unrealized. Some take a trip to Las Vegas to gamble. Some play the lottery, yet some invest in savings bonds with the expectations that the investment would be productive. If luck strikes, money will be recovered but not all the time. All in all, the disobedience to God has its heavy consequences: "By the sweat of your face shall you get bread to eat until you return to the ground from which you were taken" (Gn: 3, 19). Earning a good nest does not come easy. Perseverance, strength and patience are good ingredients in the acquisition of funds. Indeed, in order for any person to progress in spiritual or material matters, he/she must exercise great efforts. Many great accomplishments come from hard work. So, people who choose to multiply earnings must show discipline and persistence. By and large, this is something positive. In a way, it is enhancing one's potentials and one's capabilities with the help of the Lord to accomplish things. This is an important element for progress in the society of today in an era where some ideologists prefer a system that does not encourage the individual's worth rather a lifestyle that renders one dependant. Such a program denies the dignity of the human person and reduces him to a consumer who is not given a chance to produce anything good. One's dignity is reduced.

Money has become the top priority in our days. But Jesus warns us about its dangers. However, money persists to nag on some people's minds. The desire to accumulate wealth for later ease can ironically be so all consuming that you find no ease, no rest, not even in sleep. Furthermore, the accumulation of money can be the cause of conflicts, not ease can be one's only goal, thus sleep is interrupted by it. Ironically, the accumulation that takes us can be the cause or the result of conflicts. Division amongst families, friends and even globally can take its place. Jesus reminds us about the importance of being detached from money in order to preserve the bond of unity between us. Money can be a tool but it cannot satisfy everything. It allowed building the house of the Lord and, like King David did and many popes, bishops and priests. It is important to have money in order to raise a family or even to help the poor. However, despite its pivotal role in helping the poor and to have a decent life, it has not been able to offer full happiness to the human heart. The reality is that though a person may have a lot of money, no one can be exempt from hardships stemming from life itself: such as health and discord in the family. Many people, putting it simply, with a lot of money, will still go through life's tribulations. Jesus himself has warned us about the attitude we should have toward money: No man can serve two masters [...], you cannot give yourself to God and money (Mt. 6: 24). This is an invitation for us to choose God above all things and to do our best to give Him honor and glory through love and charity until He comes back. His Coming, should urge one more and more toward a profound life, rich in good works: "Sell your possessions, and give alms; provide yourselves with purses that do not grow old, with a treasure in the heavens that does not fail, where no thief approaches and no moth destroys" (Lk 12: 33). It is an invitation to use things unselfishly without thirsting for possession or control, but according to the logic of God, the logic of consideration for others which is the logic of love. In a special way, this logic is solidified in the sacrament of marriage offered to all Catholics who want to follow the Lord through a family life and who want to have their love blessed by the Lord. Only this way, couples will experience happiness and bliss in the presence of God and embrace God's teachings. We can experience the prelude of eternal life through things that are simple, pure and innocent. It is also an invitation for couples to live their married lives to comfort and to communicate and above all to respect one another without manipulation and control. Yes indeed, we all have the grace of the Holy Spirit to follow God's teachings. However, we must remain in His love and be in tune with Him. The Lord teaches us how to love. God wants us to use things and love people. Too often, people love things and use people. We will have far more impact by respecting people's dignity and fostering a culture of life than thinking money will be the ultimate solution.

We All Have Some Possessions

A s HUMAN BEINGS, IT IS easy for us to get distracted in doing so many things or engaging in so many activities that we forget what is essential. We get so caught up in many things which we believe are important, going out every day with friends, doing this or that showing our love for one another, talking on the cellular phone and no time for ourselves or for our family. With this kind of setting, family values can disappear quickly especially if there is an absence of someone who can keep the family united. All Catholic parents who, at the time of baptism, professed that they will do their best to raise and educate the children according to the Catholic values are expected to do so. The family is an important institution of the Catholic Church because the head of the Church, Jesus Christ, grew up in the Holy Family. He learned many things which allowed Him to be obedient until death. Following the steps of Jesus, family education is precious in the life of a child. A family and all of its members can work together sharing with the values that would allow them to be better people. A good family unit produces hard workers, honest, humble individuals who respect others. Such values will help change the landscape of the society filled with helplessness, injustice and pain. It is uncommon today to keep the family together, to sit down at the table and share a meal together. Sharing a meal together once a week, when every member feels and sees the importance of it, is a blessing. It is a blessing not because it allows people to be together but also it builds character, maturity and, enhances many family values. The children will observe these good practices, use them in their own family and pass them on to their own children. After the Church, the table is the place where family members share their love with each other through the sharing of the meal. It can be the best place to promote family values and to keep the family united. Sometimes, it appears easier to be loving and kind to the one who lives away from us as if those who live close to us don't want our happiness. Unable to grasp the concern of those who live close to us, young people will rush to move out of the house to join friends. Such a move allows a taste of adulthood, maturity and understanding. To a degree, such an initiative can bring something beneficial if it would land where people are discretionary to look for success. Otherwise, there will be surprises. It is easy for a young person to fall in many bad things especially if there is no supervision. Many people are not clear as to what it is in life they want to pursue. It means that a blind person cannot guide another blind person. The question is this: Why go elsewhere looking for something that is in one's midst? We encounter people who are trapped within themselves when there is a lack of self-esteem. Indeed, in the midst of confusions, life can be troubled and full of anxiety. Peace in our heart will be experienced when we recognize that we must give up some of our possessions or perhaps our love for possessions. It is a response to the call of the Lord inviting us to a life of holiness. Human attitude and perceptions can bring conflicts and misunderstandings between people. When peace is not present, there will be crisis. Unable to fix a crisis and to live in harmony, an abyss can arise between them. Deeper clashes of ideas can then separate their hearts as a result of not seeing the good or the positive in the other person. Life becomes so complicated that everything becomes complete disorder. Both communication and the positive atmosphere can no longer find their way in. It will take some change of heart from all the players involved in the conflict in order to find a common ground which will bring tranquility and reconciliation. The blaming game is a game which we all play in life. The more we play, the better we get and it goes on. The unwillingness to change is in all of us. From a biblical point of view, this is one of man's possessions, not giving it up means the denial to enter into God's Kingdom. First, it is on a personal level which will spread around. Then, these relationships can become more difficult as people refuse to change things. What we consider to be important may not if it causes conflicts. God's unchanging will is our instrument for peace. The Gospel of the Lord which is a Gospel of love and peace is the food that will nurture our desire for peace. God is the only one who can decide the reward or the punishment that a person deserves. It means that we should rely more upon God's mercy than anything else while we do our best to live a decent Christian life. As people of the world, we all have something to which we become attached and that we will not give up. We don't want to change something we perceive as good even if it separates us from others. In other words, some possessions we have may be the source of conflict between us and others but we find difficult to change it or to give it up. That is where and when we become rich. Worldly richness denies compassion and love. God has something special for each one of us. Whether we are ordinary or not, we can find such gifts when we can love more deeply. Then we can find it.

WE ARE CALLED TO DO GOOD TO OTHERS

I T IS IN THE LIGHT of today's challenges that we feel God's calling. God invites us to love one another and to welcome others. We live in an era where we encounter many individuals who prefer to have it their way. Each one of us regardless of age and status in life has issues. It's all in our make up as human beings. Although some of us believe that our lives should be spent without difficulties, we actually receive a life without crosses comparing to what the early Christians went through. There is a failure on our part, at times, to recognize God's love and power, thus seeking someone to blame. Many individuals without patience struggle deeply when things do not sway the way they see it. Yet, there are some of us who look for an easy way out of the mess we ourselves create but without patience, trust and compassion a lasting relationship would not survive. In order to prevent a disaster in the family, Catholic parents are encouraged to raise their children in a way that invites them to contemplate Jesus on the cross and learn from Him. It is essential that children living in a Catholic family setting must be taught about patience and hope when troubles and anxieties strike. It means children must be shown how to accept and handle each and every pain and helplessness. Obtaining one's rewards and joys are earned. Parents may practice consistency and constancy when painful changes take place. This requires sacrifices and communication amongst each family member. Our faith teaches us about the importance of taking up our crosses to follow the Lord. If and when there is a cross to carry, it is important to attempt and open communications talking it over and not ignoring its existence. Ignoring its existence can lead to destructive measures. It is healthier for a person to face the difficulties in life. Facing one's battle with faith and prayer is good practice because the Lord is always present in our daily life. There is an appointed time for everything. God has appointed these times. These are God's times and we pray that we recognize them appropriately. As Catholics, we must offer thanksgiving to the Lord daily and pray that He helps us during times of trouble. Indeed, Jesus continues to stay with us. He is present when we are most vulnerable and when temptations from the evil one are ready to strike. Surely, the enemy wishes to confuse us especially when our desires consist of the world. Temporary wealth and infatuations dominate our thinking: Unwanted pregnancies? Some find it easy to terminate a human life. We resort to desperation, destruction and fear. Who can forgive us when we find things unforgiveable? Only God. We constantly change our ideas, desires and attitudes. But God's everlasting love and unchanging nature will and can help us get through. It is only the cross that can demonstrate calmness and acceptance of God's will. It is up to us to look up to it in order to appreciate and love others. As we think of Jesus' last hours. Ask for God's forgiveness, speak to Him, listen as well. Yearning for God's love clears the way on how we treat others. It also clears our minds of confusion. We are all called to do good to others and it is good to continue doing it because by being good to others we glorify the Lord. The good News is that there are many good Catholics out there who are helping others tremendously. Some are helping in a visible manner, others prefer to remain anonymous. Their main purpose is to continue being Jesus in our times. Deep faith of even a little faith are the center of all this and it is essential to nurture such faith so that we become the light during the darkest times. God's everlasting love will overcome the most difficult aspects of our lives, our helplessness, our pains, our confusions and even our sins. God overcame death and He overcame the world. So, keep going with the faith. If we fall, let us start over again and don't get discouraged. With the grace of the Lord, we will get there.

THE GREATNESS OF OUR FAITH

SEEMINGLY, OUR WORLD, BECAUSE OF some of our leaders' ideologies and choices, is progressively heading to disaster. However, many of us continue to enjoy the gift of faith. Faith is something precious. It buoys our spirits to new heights when everything else has very little meaning. It is God's great gift which is personally bestowed upon the recipient. We profess our faith strongly to God when we pray the Nicene Creed. Without faith, our hearts and souls will never be at peace. Inasmuch as we are made for God, our faith is centered on God. Only the Lord can satisfy us, soothing and calming our hearts. Let us not succumb to the evil one's temptations, we may ask the Holy Spirit to guide us and request the Holy Mother's intercession for us, our families and for our own needs. Many of us struggle with God's word and what he requires in times of difficulties. As Christians and as Catholics, our guiding principles are clearly stated in the Ten Commandments. The Ten Commandments, if taken to heart can promote tranquility in our lives. Faith allows us to surrender to the Lord allowing humility and charity in our whole being. Faith allows us to embrace God's word with maturity. Our perceptions of the Gospel intensifies, thus we apply their teachings in our daily lives. As Catholics, we have been granted the Holy Sacraments which guide us: the Holy Orders for the religious or clergy, Holy Matrimony for marriage between a man and a woman. This is our faith and we must adhere to its fundamentals. No one can change or alter what they stand for, even though those who have lost the faith want to dictate their own commandements to the whole world. Therefore, a life with the Lord requires a change of heart. It requires that anyone who wants to follow the Lord must give up unbelief and doubts. The Lord imparts the sacrament of marriage to people who can live as couples. The sacrament of matrimony is a sacrament in which God allows a man and a woman in a relationship of marriage, after knowing one another who decide to culminate their relationship. Life without the gift of faith cannot endure the surprises that sometimes cause us pain and anxieties. A life with faith is a life of humility of grace of understanding and of acceptance of the cross. We can nourish our faith by doing good works, works such as assisting the needy, helping the poor, praying for those who are near death. This can also be done by attending the celebration of the Eucharist and praying the rosary. As faithful, we are encouraged to pray for priests, for the vocations and for the propagation of faith, hope and charity. Our Catholic faith shapes our lives. The Catholic teachings have been made for us and for what we become. Henceforth, we are not made for these teachings. Many remain in Church, albeit mistrusting and not comfortable with the Catechism and the Magisterium. Finding God's goodness can deepen the faith. God provides this gift without our asking and it is for us to recognize it. Our faith cheers idiosyncrasies. Our baptism is the first step when the faith was planted. We continue with our Confirmation, confirming that there is one Lord, one Baptism, one Church and all of us who are in it, worship the same God. It will take humility, changing of heart and wisdom to accept and embrace what is not seen. The faith is given to us so that we may experience life in its fullness. It is our blessing. Let us strip ourselves of our little faith, instead, let us expand it for the good of God, our neighbor and for ourselves. Let us consider that the intangible has its finite qualities - unseen but speaking in volumes. Our dignity and our identity are measured in our strong faith.

Jesus Is The First Missionary Given To The World

J ESUS IS THE SOURCE AND foundation of all missions. He is himself the mission because He was sent by God to bring peace and to show the whole world the path that leads to salvation. It is through the Church that His mission continues to exist. Because of that particular identity of His being, before anything else, any person who wants to go to the mission to help others must enter in a relationship with the Lord Jesus. It means that no one can start a missionary activity whether it is feeding the poor, visiting the prisoners or serving in any pastoral branch of the Church if that person does not have the humility to learn from Jesus and accomplish the task that has been given to him. It means that the service a faithful wants to offer to God in the community must be in harmony with the mission of Jesus who came not to do His will rather the will of God the Father. Because of that responsibility of the faithful to continue the work of Jesus, many men and women desire to help others particularly the poor in many social or religious organizations like the Peace Corps, St. Vincent de Paul, Catholic Charities etc.[…]. Others feel the need to go to other countries to respond to their call to the mission. Because of that possibility, priest, nuns, brothers have given up their families and many other realities of life to become a missionary. Some other people will offer their time, their talents and their resources with the purpose of continuing the mission started by Jesus. However, there can be mission or voluntary work only if a person accepts to be governed by the words of God encountered in the Scriptures to which the Church has been given the role of guardian. When the faithful accepts to be led by the words of God, his example of life brings about peace wherever he/she is. That is the reason why, it is important to make room in our life for improvement in our faith so that we all become instruments of peace. Only this way, will we be followers of Jesus. Peace means to be obedient to the Father and to do our best to choose Him as our daily bread. Peace means also to have an attitude that encourages unity and not division. It also calls us to an attitude where charity becomes part of our daily activity, always ready to help another with the purpose of keeping the legacy started by Jesus. The obedience that is requested is not an act of blind faith without asking questions especially when things are not clear and obvious. The obedience required by the Lord invites us to ask questions not with the purpose of diminishing the faith but rather to understand things better and to bring peace in our heart and around us. When a mission is not quite clear, it can only encourage confusion. In other words, every single baptized person has the responsibility to make known the name of the Lord in a way he tries to understand every day the reason why he/she was created by God and to be present in this particular society or in this particular community with a particular mission. It means that it is important for a person to know his mission. He/she will know that mission only when he/she is willing to walk behind Jesus and His Church and not behind those who are the enemies of the faith. Not everyone in the world will be open and ready to follow Jesus and continue His mission. In the same way, not everyone who is a baptized person will be an instrument of peace. Sometimes, we may be scandalized by people who are involved in the Church in the way they fail to welcome, to be honest, to support the poor and to be obedient to the Magisterium. They may even fail to give the testimony that everyone is waiting for. In that aspect, the recent sexual scandal committed by some members of the clergy around the world should not be an occasion to disregard the importance and the validity of the mission of Jesus entrusted to the Church. On the contrary, His mission of peace invites to continue to pray so that the mission becomes a group effort and not the responsibility of a few. Prayer is the key to resolve all problems whether they may be on the material, interpersonal or spiritual level. We must pray when we are persecuted and also the times of conflicts and division. By doing so, we will contribute to peace that the Lord came to bring on earth.

We Must Acknowledge Our Dependency Upon God

A T A TIME WHEN THE Catholic message is not a part of the mainstream of the liberal mindset, the Church has little means to defend itself. As Catholics, our role is to have the awareness of our perceptions, behaviors and attitudes. We are somewhat different in that we are the soul of the world. Freedom of expression and speech have become our vehicles in our daily routines. Christian virtues have taken a backseat, neglected and forgotten. Virtues are essential in the life of a Christian and must be observed and nurtured. They are manifestations of God's being. Virtues govern and provide temperance. Some virtues are gifts as early as birth, others are learned through daily experiences and others are obtained through retreats, reading of the scriptures, prayers and meditations. Learning is ongoing: listening to homilies brings new challenges from the scriptures. The Catechism and the Magisterium of the Catholic Church expand our knowledge giving us virtues. As a result, we can experience the peace of the Lord in our hearts. Man in his existence must practice virtue. It allows us to practice temperance and control of our emotions. The role of the Church is to interpret God's messages, clarify and perhaps, simplify God's message of peace and love. We the faithful base our daily lives on God's precepts. The presence of virtues allows human beings to be respectful to one another. If conflicts arise virtues of self control, humility, perseverance and charity provide thoughts of quietude and backing off. All in all we cannot help but be humble, able to accept our own limitations thus denying ourselves. Many of us learned the golden rule at a very young age, thus strong foundation of respect for God, and for others. Happiness is possible if we have a strong faith. If we live our life obedient to the faith, we have a better chance to be at peace with God and ourselves. As we grow in the faith, it is best to keep and observe our gifts of virtues inborn or acquired. Strong faith as a virtue keeps us in line, reminding us that everything has its place and its right time. Surrendering to God and depending upon Him erases our doubts. Virtues are awareness, reminders and whispers from God. Among the numerous virtues that we are encouraged to acquire and develop in our spiritual journey as Catholics, humility is the most challenging one. The challenge comes from the fact that as human persons, we have a self appreciation of ourselves. At an extreme level, we are not apt to follow directions. We have elevated ourselves and it can be very detrimental. An example is when a child is manifesting inappropriate behaviors and a parent overlooks such behaviors. It may be that a neighbor finds a way to express comments about these behaviors. Conflicts can arise between the parent, the neighbor and the child. Communication lines are non-existent. Nevertheless, if virtues such as humility, faith in the Lord and peace of heart exist, then there can be love and an unnecessary conflict can be avoided. From a spiritual point of view, the advice given to us can be a message from the Holy Spirit and our guardian angel is delivering it to us but we fail to recognize its importance. As Christians, peace of heart is attainable when and if we accept our challenges as good learning experiences. They allow us to grow emotionally and mentally. But, once we embrace this virtue and it becomes a part of our repertoire, patience, acceptance and happiness in life will develop. Many of us struggle when we are impatient. But, with patience, we can help save many relationships. Our blessings are many when we remain humble like Mary, the Mother of God. Humility is the recognition that no matter what our accomplishments, we still stand in need of the Lord. God hears the cry of the poor and of the oppressed, especially those who acknowledge their dependency on him. Having heard Paul's cries for help, the Lord crowned him with eternal salvation. We must remember to surrender our everyday activities, prayers, joys and sufferings to the Lord. After all, we belong to Him.

The Lord Comes To Visit Us

THE LORD WANTS TO VISIT us and how can we prepare a place for Him in our hearts? This is the constant challenge of our daily life: to prepare a place for the Lord and embellish the tabernacle of our hearts where He may stay to protect and guard us. When the Lord visits a person, His purpose is to give a particular mission to that person for his spiritual well being or for the sake of an entire community. This is a time where that person needs to do something that will change his life. This is a time for conversion, a time to love God and to love his neighbors. It will require a lot of generosity of the heart to put everything away and be totally available to listen to the Master. We must be there for Him. Otherwise, we may become distracted by being involved in so many things that we ignore His presence. It means that, in our spiritual journey, we all will have to pause a while in order to welcome the Lord who knocks at our door. It requires from us a clean heart where we do our best to be at peace with God and those around us. It is so easy to fall into conflict with other people and then to hold grudges. Prayer is the key for us to be people of peace wherever we are. It is important to grow day by day and to learn from our mistakes with the purpose of experiencing peace and happiness. It is so good to be at peace with everyone in our household. It is a communal effort, it is a team work. Everyone should be involved: both parents and children where there is a family. If there is not a family, the effort must be directed to the neighbors or those who are our friends. Maturity can be essential also for a person to be a promoter of peace. Maturity means wisdom not to waste energy in negativity and to realize that the days are given to us to enjoy and not to be in division. Yes indeed, wherever there are human beings, misunderstandings may occur. However, they should not last for days where the environment becomes heavy and where communication is broken. Nevertheless, it will take maturity at all levels for a person not to hold grudges and be quick to reconcile. It means also not to pay attention to things that may lead to problems rather to promote positivity in the relationship because the Lord is in our hearts. Whenever there are problems, we are called to offer them to the Lord. It is better to let the Lord resolve them instead of trying to be the person who speaks his mind or who is not afraid to talk. Sometimes, it is better to be silent and not say a word. These principles are essential in every community, household and any relationship. They must be respected and have to go on all the time. By doing so, we will express our detachment to those possessions of the world that cannot give us peace. In the eyes of the world, such way of life can be considered as repression of our own freedom; while in a spiritual point of view, it will be considered as maturity in the faith. The human will is weak and wounded by sin, the search for peace therefore demands from each individual constant control of the passions particularly pride and anger. Zaccheus was a rich man in terms of material possessions; but, he needed something else that only Jesus could give to him. He searched for the Lord with the sincerity of the heart with the purpose of receiving something special from Him. The Lord paid attention to his desire by responding to him that He will go to his house. In the same manner, we are encouraged to go to the Lord, to look for Him and ask him to go to our house, both internal and external. There, tell Him all our miseries particularly those that make us prisoners of many possessions. This is the time to get rid of all grudges so that we become free in the Lord. This is the time to let it go. It is a very good opportunity to face the resentment we carry within ourselves and to recovery. Recovery is important in the life of a person for the fact when we are not in good shape we become cowards. That is where we become vulnerable, we become angry quickly and unable to refresh ourselves. By searching for the Lord, we will allow ourselves to be drawn into His words. The Lord wants to draw us to himself so that we may remain in His goodness. No matter how sinful we can feel, the Lord can make miracles. The Lord can change things in our being. He can give us enough strength to turn away from our many temptations. The Lord knows how to receive us with all our dirtiness and make us the temple of the Holy Spirit for everyone to see and enjoy.

OUR LIFE ON EARTH
IS NOT FOREVER

AS WE GET CLOSE TO the end of the liturgical year, the Church invites us to reflect on the brevity of our lives here on earth. It is a subject which we, as human persons, must take into consideration. No one is eternal. Our temporary status is not to and should not frighten us. Everything that the Lord wills is for our good. Our Lord provides us tools, good perceptions, courage and His love. The awareness in which we embrace our own demise proves healthy. By the grace of our Lord, we build better and more wholesome relationships with God and with our family members. Good treatments with our fellow human beings can bring a lot of strength to face the challenges of the daily life. From a spiritual point of view, it does not really matter the number of years each one of us may have, we can instill in ourselves and others a life of liturgy where God's life is celebrated constantly. We can learn that God's will is a source of strength and love. Such a celebration that is God's life can lead us to the full realization of the covenant between God and humanity. It is pure and simple that our daily lives are a blessing in which we receive and we give. God's blessings are so abundant. Keeping these blessings to ourselves is not enough. The Lord wishes us to share them and to pass our talents and treasures along. Each and every one of us has a gift to share. It can be a smile, a sincere greeting, offering to help with chores when someone is ill. Other ways are to give drink to the thirsty and yes to pray for the dead. God has outlined the corporal works of mercy for us. Our lives are better lived when we can extend the spiritual work of mercy such as comforting the sorrowful, bearing wrongs patiently, forgiving all injuries and praying for those who are in need. Let us not allow ourselves to delve in our own crosses and our predicaments. Let us open up to others around us and let us also sympathize with their troubles and their anxieties. The principles and virtues of our Catholic faith remind us to always greet people and acknowledge their presence at any time and any place. By doing so, we will greet God's presence in them. Let us have the eyes of one who loves. Parents are encouraged to instill these same values to their children. In turn, such effects permeate in everyone politeness, kindness and respect which are a few good manners not complicated to learn. No one is perfect but good practices please God very much. Being consistent and faithful are very pleasing to God. The way we grow in God's ways is to focus and strengthen our faith and ourselves by doing things that God desires. We can alert ourselves by doing them now and not later. We can also show our love and our appreciation to others when they are alive and not wait till after death to express our concern and our care instead of purchasing expensive flowers to be placed on one's coffin later on. The Lord summons us to celebrate the presence of our friends and families while they are alive and together we will experience peace and understanding. Jesus told us again and again to love one another as he has loved us. His life was spent with great compassion for the humble, the sick and the troubled. Jesus' advice to follow Him will allow His followers to share the joys and blessings of the life to come. He will bring these souls to His intimacy so that they will experience eternal life. It means that the city that we have here on earth is not a lasting city. We await in glory the eternal city that is the city of God. Therefore, let us abandon ourselves to the Lord, to His Church and to the faith.

Even If We Are Betrayed, We Must Remain Faithful

I T IS A GOOD THING for a person to have love in his heart. God is love and if we are followers of Jesus, it is logical that we learn how to cultivate love in our lives so that we may become another Christ to everyone we meet. Love is a tough thing. It is not easy to love even though some people believe it is. The difficulty lies in that love requires one's life to become one's gift to others. In a sacramental marriage, there is a conjugal relationship between a husband and his wife. Through understanding and dialogue, they unite and grow together. This type of unity encourages honesty and humility thus allowing both to be one. Void of openness and affection between spouses or between friends and families, a good relationship cannot emerge; it will cause more pain than happiness. A true human love will last until death while the divine love lasts forever. Love is nurtured with God's love through learning His words and receiving His sacraments. Without this essential food to keep us focused, all love can be there for a while and disappear at the first difficulty. God loves what is intangible while the world loves pride, status, honor and whatever is tangible. That is the reason why it is important for couples to renew their love to each other every day of their lives in order to continue making their lives a gift to each other. Friends and families can discover a deeper commitment when every aspect of life is surrendered to the Lord. Praying together, coming to Mass and dining as a family allow many love relationships to survive. Love means to be open to other relationships where so much can be acquired and learned. Exclusion of others and closeness impedes growth. Being forgiving and truthful are true ingredients of acceptance. Love requires also that you accept that your family or your friend tells you the truth. The one who loves will also control his tongue in order to avoid words that might hurt you. In addition, he will always say the truth to you. Sometimes we may not want to hear it. However, it is the truth. Through love, God created the whole world and all that is in it. Through love, we also are encouraged to continue the mission of love so that we may bring some comfort and care to others. Love builds character and it allows people to deny prejudices and predilections. Love provides a feeling of security and strength to bear our crosses and sufferings. Peace and happiness are the end results of the love we experience. As any other thing for the development of a person, love is an education, something that is obtained at home. It has to be manifested and expressed in all the little details of daily life. A child who grows up amongst loving individuals will become a loving adult. As the child blossoms to adulthood, he/she manifests toward his fellow human beings what he/she has learned at home and ultimately towards his/her lifetime spouse. The cycle begins and hopefully continues with the same love that he/she learned from home. Parents are the role model and must show to their children the right path to take for a good and virtuous life. It is important to remember that a love that has experienced betrayal and still exists is a powerful love that contains depth and quality. It is a gift from the Lord. Jesus loves us this way and it is to this kind of love that we are called to. The reality is our inheritance from our first parents, Adam and Eve allows us to experience the pains of original sin which in itself is the source of our test. We can feel it in our sufferings, our illnesses, our tragedies and our daily trials. As God's children, we are given these difficulties, they are ways we can share Jesus' sufferings. However, there is no human life without the test. It means that everyone who is a descendant of Adam will experience the consequences of the original sins in its life. It also means, that as human persons, we can expect to be tested. It will be presented either via illness coming from the human body, part of our nature or through the contact we have with people such as persecution, betrayal or deception. If we remain in the Lord, there will be fewer temptations to follow the path of the enemy and discouragement. We should never be distracted from the Lord's presence in our lives. This is the reason why He came to lead us to a life of hope in all the problems we may face.

Jesus Christ, A King Not Like The Kings Of This World

THE KINGSHIP OF JESUS IS a mystery which no human person will ever be able to fathom. It is so deep-rooted that the human capacity of comprehending things is beyond measure. Because of its richness and its message to the whole of humanity, only faith allows us to enter this broad and supernatural reality. Though such a title might offend many people and provoke distractions, frustrations and perplexities as experienced by the Jews in Jesus' time, the Kingdom of Jesus brings a new order into our lives calling us to a life of obedience, service and humility. Jesus Christ is a true King: the King of kings, however the Gospel presents His Kingdom in a manner that can really battle the one who is not in an intimacy with the Lord. In the scriptures, His power is taken away by the rulers of this world. They judged Him, they stripped and crucified Him. In addition, on the cross, He is deprived from any freedom and from any liberty of action. The only thing He had was His voice which He used to turn to His Father asking for support and help, and to offer forgiveness to those who crucified Him. What a contrast between this Jesus who cured the sick and the Jesus who had the power to change the water into wine and now on the cross: He cannot save himself? Such presentation of a King is a scandal for those whose faith is weak and are unable to understand the path of renouncement chosen by Jesus to offer the supreme offering of Himself to the Father. It has nothing in common with the rest of the human kings living in their palaces and castles with no contact with their people. Jesus accepted to lose all his rights and die on the cross for us men and for our salvation. With such a gesture of sacrifice, He is the true shepherd who gives His life for His sheep. It is the triumph of love and goodness and the proof that He is King. By using the madness of man expressed in His crucifixion, to the accomplishment of His good Will, allowing the hatred of the crowd to contribute to His act of love, Jesus is not any kind of man, He is God. He came to prepare us so that we may follow His example. Those who want to enter into His Kingdom are invited to take up their crosses of life and to follow Him into that path of obedience to the Father. Such a request on the part of Jesus is a mystery that will be understood only by those who put their trust in Him. It is a difficult task that will require a lot of humility and the desire to do the will of the Father. Nevertheless, it is this particularity and the uniqueness of this paradox that is at the crossroad of the Christian faith. It constitutes the sign of His mission and the source of salvation for us who will turn to the Father in every moment of darkness that we may encounter in our spiritual journey. So, the Kingdom of Jesus is a Kingdom of love so that anyone who receives the gift of faith in his life must choose to walk in the path of love following Jesus. It is this attitude that will bring security and comfort to the soul of the faithful wherever he may be. Remember the thief on the cross: he was saved by faith which invites him to an attitude of humility. He recognized his sins and turned to Jesus for mercy. The same day, he was with Jesus Christ in paradise. If we have not done it yet, it is the season to ask the Lord to bless us with the gift of humility and ask Him to forgive us for our sins. This is the way we will experience the joy of paradise.

THE CHURCH OF THE LORD
IS A CHURCH OF LAW

IT IS EASY TO FORGET that the Church is the consequence and the continuation of the encounter between God and Moses which occurred at Mount Sinai where God gave Moses the Ten Commandments to lead His people toward the Kingdom. While this encounter in the Church is happening now between God and us, the Lord Jesus gives the same task to the Church commanding her to proclaim the truth to the world so that everyone recognizes that there is no other source of happiness for human beings except in Him. It is an important responsibility on the part of the Church and at the same time it is a privilege for us to be given such a direction in order not to be lost and confused. This is the reason why the laws in the Church must be accepted as guides and directions for us. They are to be seen as signs of love for all of us and not as a source for doubt and anger. It is so common for some people to see the laws of the Church as an impediment to their freedom and their happiness. How many times we hear people saying that the laws of the Church are man's laws and therefore you don't need these laws to express your love to God. The truth is that the laws of the Church are in continuity with the Ten Commandments and through them we are called to express our love to God because the Church is the Church of the Lord. The Laws of the Church are to be considered as the laws of the Lord based on the authority the Lord Jesus gave to the apostles: "Whatever you bind on earth will be bound in Heaven". To this statement, the Lord says: "If you love me you will keep my Commandments[…]. Anybody who receives my commandments and keeps them will be one who loves me" (John 14: 15-21). But, in order for us to know God, to worship Him and to listen to Him, the Church is the only institution given to us to promote and enhance our relationship with the Father. It means that the Church has the mission to make known and to spread the message of God contained in the Ten Commandments. In doing so, the Church gives us all the possibility to receive the divine blessings in our lives.

It means that an encounter with God can only be possible within a context of law encountered in the Ten Commandments. Consequently, no matter the negative opinions people may have toward the laws of the Church, the reality is that the Church is a Church of Law. The challenge for the believers in today's society is to trust that the Commandments are more than ten statements given to the entire world. They are like chapters that need to be developed or decoded. Everything is said in them but in a condensed manner. The details are all spread throughout the Scriptures in both the Old and the New Testaments. If a believer looks only at the ten statements given in the commandments to reject the laws of the Church regarding the reception of the Sacraments and many issues concerning the conduct of a baptized person, he/she will always say such laws are man's laws as a way to reject them. However, it is not fair to say that some of the Church's laws are not in the commandments without exploring the contents of the Bible and its relationship and the connection related to the laws of the Church and the Scriptures. Nonetheless, the laws are aimed to guide and protect us in order to experience happiness and life everlasting. Their purpose is to help us serve God in a better manner and to walk in the right path. In other words, with the laws in the Church, we all will know what to do and the risk for injustice to God can be very minimal particularly if we listen to the voice of the Holy Spirit.

In addition, it is accurate to believe that the Church is more than a human organization even though the hierarchy in it is composed of many men with their strengths and weaknesses. However, the laws of the Church impeding women to be priests, or a lay person to have authority over a cleric, or divorced people remarried by civil law or living with a partner without marriage by the Church to have access to communion should not be considered as man's laws. The laws of the Church stating that the faithful who desire a family life must be married by the Church are part of the Ten Commandments. We are the temple of the Holy Spirit and if we have a partner without receiving the sacrament of marriage in the Catholic Church, the humility of the faith will encourage us to come back to God and follow His commandments. Such an initiative will allow us to experience peace in our hearts because the sacraments were created for those who will follow the Lord in His Church. It is important to feed ourselves with the mystery that is present in the makeup of the Church in the line of Abraham, Isaac and Jacob. It is the responsibility of the faithful to make the effort to complete his/her education in the faith to be more humble to accept the mystery of salvation. The foundation in which we are called to understand the Church is more than what we see with our eyes and is also more than what our perception is. Before all else, the Church is a mystery that goes beyond our rights. To benefit from it in an abundant and fruitful manner, we should never approach it with our merely human interpretation.